CLAIRE THOMSON
The 5 O'Clock Apron

One Pan
CHICKEN

**70 All-in-One Chicken Recipes
For Simple Meals, Every Day**

photography by Sam Folan

Hardie Grant

QUADRILLE

One for all my brilliant friends,
especially those who ask, 'Help, what
shall I cook for dinner this evening?'

Introduction

There are many chicken dishes from all over the world and I can confidently say that choosing just 70 recipes to feature in this book has been a challenging task, ruthless even. I could easily have gone on: 100 recipes, 1000 recipes, more! One simple principle has helped to hone this selection process, and it is the title: *One Pan Chicken*. Is the recipe doable and delicious, and can it be cooked in just one pan? If so, yes, it's in this book, making *One Pan Chicken* an essential collection of crowd-pleasing chicken recipes. Each recipe you choose to cook will undoubtedly be your new favourite chicken dish... until, that is, you cook the next.

A popular ingredient, chicken is as much a grocery favourite for midweek, minimal-fuss dinners as it is for more indulgent, celebratory weekend cooking. The versatility of chicken is very much its selling point. Stating the obvious, we should all be buying the best-quality chicken our budget can buy, with free range and/or organic chicken being the ideal. A responsibly sourced whole chicken will cost you, as such I would urge you to be scrupulous in its demolition. Use one of the whole-bird recipes in this book, and after eating your fill, strip the carcass, prizing every single morsel from the frame to use in one of the leftovers recipes in the last chapter, a fine end to a good chicken. If less expense than buying a whole bird is necessary, perhaps cooking for fewer people or less of an occasion, I've listed the most common cuts of chicken available to buy in the butcher's and at the supermarket to use in many of the recipes. If you are buying chicken from a butcher, a good one should be happy to help with any of your butchery needs, spatchcocking a whole bird, for example. If not, as ever, there are countless tutorials to show you how to do this online.

In many of the recipes, I've suggested you use either chicken legs, thighs or drumsticks, interchangeable cuts of chicken and all with good flavour and a fairly forgiving margin when it comes to cookery timings. But the choice is yours – which cut do you prefer to use? Choose your favourite, then make the recipe your own. As for chicken breasts, some chicken recipes are simply better when made with breast meat – not all, but some – and these recipes specifically call for breast in the ingredients. Chicken wings and drumsticks are the cheapest cut of chicken to buy, so, if you really do love to cook and eat chicken, a teetering plate of either, all cooked to sticky perfection, will be as much a celebration of chicken as it is to your excellent and thrifty cookery skills.

I cook and write about food for a living, and never in my 10 years of writing cookery books has the question 'What are you working on at the moment?' elicited such a predictable and glowing response. It has even taken me by surprise. In summary of these conversations – and there have been plenty in and around the time I've been writing, from parents who are friends at the school gates, to chef friends, my local butcher, my publishers of course, and also my mum and all of her friends – people want to eat chicken, and they want to cook that chicken simply in one pan and they want that chicken to be absolutely delicious. I think that's doable, and here's how.

CASSEROLE

Chicken with Cannellini Beans, Tomatoes, Cream and Dijon Mustard

Serves 4

1kg (2lb 4oz) whole skin-on chicken
  breasts, thighs, legs or drumsticks
2 tbsp olive oil
250g (9oz) cherry tomatoes, halved
4 garlic cloves, finely chopped
30g (1oz) butter
150ml (5fl oz) dry white wine
200ml (7fl oz) double (heavy) cream
1½ tbsp Dijon mustard
2 x 400g (14oz) cans of cannellini (white)
  or butter beans, drained and rinsed
a big pinch of ground nutmeg
1 small bunch of tarragon, or use flat-leaf
  parsley or basil, leaves roughly chopped
salt and freshly ground black pepper

Chicken breasts work best for this recipe, though you can use thighs or legs instead. Cannellini beans are one of my favourite beans to cook with – a creamy canvas of flavour, the beans soaking up everything and all this recipe has to offer. This dish also freezes well.

1. Season the chicken with salt and pepper.

2. Heat the oil in a casserole pan over a moderate-high heat, add the chicken and brown all over for about 5 minutes each side, until coloured and beginning to cook through. Then, add the tomatoes and cook for 5 minutes more until the tomatoes are soft and collapsed. Stir in the garlic and the butter and cook for 1 minute, until fragrant.

3. Add the white wine and cook for 5 minutes, until the liquid in the pan has thickened, turning the chicken every now and then.

4. Add the cream, Dijon mustard, beans and nutmeg and stir to combine. Season generously with salt and freshly ground black pepper. When the mixture begins to bubble around the edges, reduce the heat to low and let it simmer, stirring occasionally, for 10–15 minutes, turning the chicken every now and then, until the sauce has thickened and the chicken is cooked through.

5. Check the seasoning, adding a touch more salt and freshly ground black pepper to taste, then stir through the herbs. Serve immediately.

Chicken Pilaf

Serves 4

700g (1lb 9oz) boneless, skinless chicken
   (thigh is best), diced
30g (1oz) butter or ghee, or 2 tbsp
   vegetable, sunflower or groundnut oil
2 bay leaves, scrunched a little
4 cloves
1 cinnamon stick (about 10cm/4in)
1 heaped tsp cumin seeds
1 onion, finely diced
2 garlic cloves, peeled and finely chopped
1 tsp ground coriander
½ tbsp ground cumin
1 x 400g (14oz) can of chickpeas
   (garbanzos), drained and rinsed
200g (7oz) spinach, washed and cut into
   broad ribbons; or use baby spinach
300g (10½oz) basmati rice
500ml (17fl oz) hot water or stock
   (chicken or vegetable)
1 lemon: ½ finely sliced for topping;
   ½ cut into quarters, to serve
1 small bunch of dill, leaves roughly
   chopped
salt and freshly ground black pepper
plain yogurt seasoned with salt, to serve
sumac for sprinkling, to serve

I'm taking inspiration from Turkey for this pilaf, a favourite family meal. The liquid and the rice cooking time in the recipe means that chicken thighs or legs are the ideal cut to use, with the meat cooking to tender perfection. You must then hope for a good crunchy layer of golden rice on the bottom of your casserole pan – this is the prize that must be shared or wolfed with a greedy abandon (in Persian cooking it is called the tahdig).

1. Season the chicken with salt and pepper.

2. Heat the butter, ghee or oil in a casserole pan over a moderate heat. Add the chicken, browning all over for around 5 minutes, then add the bay leaves, cloves, cinnamon stick and cumin seeds and fry for about 30 seconds more, until the cumin is aromatic and the spices have flavoured the butter.

3. Add the onion and cook for around 8–10 minutes, until soft and translucent. Add the garlic and continue to cook for 2 minutes more, until fragrant.

4. Add the ground coriander and ground cumin together with a big pinch of salt and cook for 1 minute more, stirring all the while.

5. Add the drained chickpeas (garbanzos) and the spinach, stir well to incorporate and cook for 2 minutes, until any excess moisture from the spinach has evaporated.

6. Stir in the rice and then add the hot water or stock. Bring to a boil, season once more with salt and pepper to taste, add the lemon slices to the top, then cover the casserole pan with a tight-fitting lid and continue to cook over a low-moderate heat for around 20–25 minutes, until the rice is cooked through and the liquid has all but evaporated. Ideally, if you carefully check, on the bottom of the pan, a crust of scorched or crispy, golden brown rice will have formed.

7. Remove the pan from the heat, fluff the cooked rice with a fork and strew all over with the chopped dill.

8. Serve with the lemon wedges and some seasoned yogurt sprinkled with sumac at the table, keeping an eye out for any whole spices, and discarding them as you go.

Chicken and Leek Pot Pie

Serves 4

For the pastry (or use a 320g/11oz ready-rolled sheet of shortcrust pastry)

100g (3½oz) very cold butter, cut into very small cubes
200g (7oz) plain (all-purpose) flour, plus more to dust
½ tsp salt
1 small egg, beaten

For the filling

2 tbsp olive oil
600g (1lb 5oz) boneless, skinless chicken (thigh is best), diced (or the same weight of leftover cooked chicken – simply add it towards the end of cooking the pie filling, with enough time to heat through)
30g (1oz) butter
300g (10½oz) leeks, trimmed and pale green and white cut into 5mm (¼in) slices
2 garlic cloves, finely chopped
2 tbsp plain (all-purpose) flour
300ml (10½fl oz) chicken stock, or use dry white wine
150ml (5fl oz) double (heavy) cream
2 tsp thyme leaves
½ small bunch of flat-leaf parsley or tarragon, leaves finely chopped
2 tbsp Dijon mustard
salt and freshly ground black pepper

Use chicken thigh or leftover cooked chicken to make this pie. Chicken stock is ideal to create the rich sauce, thickened with a roux – but you can use dry white wine if you don't have any stock to hand. I've given the recipe for pastry here, but in the spirit of one pan, use store-bought shortcrust if you like.

1. Make the pastry, if needed. Using your fingertips or a food processor, rub the butter into the flour and salt until it resembles breadcrumbs, then add 2 tablespoons of very cold water until the dough comes together. Remove it from the food processor, if using, and then knead gently on your work surface until just smooth, taking care to not overwork it. Shape the dough into a disc, wrap it in cling film and chill while you make the filling.

2. Heat the olive oil in a casserole pan over a moderate heat. Add the chicken and a big pinch of salt and brown the meat, stirring often, for about 5 minutes, until nicely bronzed in parts. Put the part-cooked chicken on a plate and wipe out the casserole pan.

3. Preheat the oven to 200°C/180°C fan/400°F/Gas 6.

4. Melt the butter in the pan over a moderate–low heat. Add the leeks and cook for around 10 minutes, until very, very soft. Add the garlic and cook for 2 minutes more, until fragrant. Add the 2 tablespoons of flour and cook for 1 minute more.

5. Add the chicken back to the pan, then add the chicken stock and cream, turn up the heat to high and bring to a simmer, stirring all the time. Reduce the heat to moderate and cook the pie filling for around 10 minutes, until the chicken is cooked through. Keep an eye on the pan, stirring occasionally to ensure the sauce doesn't catch. Remove the pan from the heat and stir in the herbs, mustard and salt and pepper to taste. Set aside.

6. Roll out the pastry to 1cm (½in) thick (unless using ready-rolled). Then, cut the pastry to size, so that the pastry lid covers the pie filling in the pan. Lay the pastry on top of the filling and cut a small air vent. Brush the top with beaten egg.

7. Bake the pie in the oven for 30 minutes, until the pastry is golden brown and crisp, and the pie filling is bubbling hot. Allow the pie to rest for around 5 minutes before serving.

Madras Chicken Curry Serves 4

50g (1¾oz) butter or ghee, or 50ml
  vegetable, sunflower or groundnut oil
1 tbsp brown mustard seeds
1 large onion, finely chopped
4 garlic cloves, thinly sliced
1 heaped tbsp grated (shredded) fresh
  ginger (skin-on is fine)
2–4 small whole green chillies, to taste
10 fresh curry leaves, or use dried
  (optional but recommended)
1–2 tsp hot chilli powder, to taste
  (or use a mild chilli powder if you
  want less heat)
1 x 400g (14oz) can of tomatoes, blended
  until smooth (or use passata/strained
  tomatoes), mixed with 100ml (3½fl oz)
  water and a big pinch of sugar
juice of 1 lemon
1 tsp salt
700g (1lb 9oz) boneless, skinless chicken
  (thigh is best), diced
2 tsp garam masala
freshly ground black pepper

With its deep red, spicy sauce made with tomatoes and onions, this is an extremely popular dish in Indian restaurants and takeaways. The name refers to the city of Chennai (once Madras), where it represents just one style of many different curry sauces (as documented by British inhabitants of the city c.1639 and beyond). With no historically definitive version of Madras curry, we must assume that modern-day recipes are the origin of British Indian chefs and restaurant owners. The caveat clear, this recipe draws influence from Madras curries that I have eaten here in the UK. I think diced boneless chicken thigh works best here. Plain cooked rice or Indian flat breads and an assortment of jarred Indian pickles make good accompaniments. This dish will freeze well.

1. Heat the butter, ghee or oil in a casserole pan over a moderate heat. Add the mustard seeds and fry for around 30 seconds, until they begin to sizzle and pop. Add the onion and fry for around 10 minutes until softened, even turning lightly golden is good.

2. Add the garlic, ginger, whole green chillies and curry leaves and fry for 1 minute, or until aromatic. Add the chilli powder and fry for 1 minute more, then stir in the blended tomato mixture and half the lemon juice, and add the salt and plenty of freshly ground black pepper. Simmer the lot for around 5 minutes, until rich and reduced.

3. Add the diced chicken and continue to cook over a moderate heat with a lid on for around 15–20 minutes, until the chicken is cooked through. Check the seasoning, adjusting with some extra salt if necessary, the remaining lemon juice and plenty of ground black pepper to taste. Scatter over the garam masala, the heat of the sauce jump-starting this fragrant spice blend to season the finished curry. Remove the pan from the heat and serve.

Chicken Tagine with Chickpeas, Dates and Apricots

Serves 4

1 small bunch of flat-leaf parsley, leaves roughly chopped

1 small bunch of coriander (cilantro), leaves roughly chopped

4 garlic cloves, thinly sliced

1 small, preserved lemon, seeds removed, skin and flesh finely chopped

5 tbsp olive oil

1kg (2lb 4oz) whole chicken thighs, legs or drumsticks

big pinch of saffron

2 tbsp warm water

2 onions, thinly sliced

3 carrots, peeled and thinly sliced

3 ripe tomatoes, thinly sliced, or use whole plum from a can, roughly chopped

1 tsp ground cumin

½ tsp freshly ground black pepper

1 tsp ground turmeric

1 tsp ground coriander

1 tsp ground ginger

½ tsp salt, plus more to taste

2 x 400g (14oz) cans of chickpeas (garbanzos), drained and rinsed

50g (1¾oz) dried dates, pitted and roughly chopped

50g (1¾oz) dried apricots, roughly chopped

juice of ½ lemon

50g (1¾oz) pitted green olives, roughly chopped

harissa, to serve

cooked couscous, to serve (optional)

A tagine can be the vessel used to cook the meat, in this case chicken, or refer to the finished dish itself. The key here is using some of the preserved lemon, coriander and garlic to marinate the chicken, ensuring a deeply flavoured meat that can rival alongside the saffron, dates and ground ginger. This is a dish about building layers of flavour on flavour. Good store-bought harissa is a fine accompaniment for the melting and tender chicken.

1. Blend or finely chop the parsley and half the coriander (cilantro) with half the garlic, half the preserved lemon and 2 tablespoons of the olive oil to a coarse purée.

2. Mix the marinade with the chicken, cover and leave to marinate in the fridge for at least 1 hour, although overnight is ideal. Remove the chicken from the fridge about 20 minutes before you plan to cook it. Alternatively, forgo the marinating time and continue with the method below.

3. Soak the saffron strands in the 2 tablespoons of warm water.

4. Heat the remaining olive oil in a casserole pan, or use a heatproof tagine if you have one, over a moderate heat. Add the onions, remaining garlic, the carrots, tomatoes and ground spices and the ½ teaspoon of salt to the olive oil, to soften and turn fragrant – around 10 minutes should do.

5. Add the chickpeas (garbanzos) and the dried fruit to the pan.

6. Arrange the marinated chicken on top and sprinkle over the saffron and its soaking water. Add the remaining preserved lemon, the lemon juice and the olives. Pour over 200ml (7fl oz) of water, place a lid on the pan and then simmer very gently over a moderate-low heat for about 45 minutes, until the chicken is meltingly tender and cooked through.

7. Remove from the heat and allow to rest for 15 minutes, then season to taste and top with the remaining chopped coriander and the harissa. Serve with cooked couscous, if you like.

Chicken with Pumpkin and Sesame Seed Almond Mole

Serves 4

2 dried ancho chillies, deseeded
   (recommended)
2 pasilla chillies, deseeded
   (recommended)
2 guajillo chillies, deseeded
   (recommended)
50g (1¾oz) raisins or sultanas
boiling water from a kettle
30g (1oz) pumpkin seeds
50g (1¾oz) whole blanched almonds
30g (1oz) sesame seeds
15 cherry tomatoes
1 onion, peeled and cut into 6 wedges
6 garlic cloves, peeled
½ tsp salt
½ tsp freshly ground black pepper
1 tsp dried Mexican oregano
   (recommended), or use 1 tsp
   dried oregano
¼ tsp ground fennel or anise
½ tsp ground cinnamon
4 tbsp olive oil, or neutral oil, such as
   vegetable, sunflower or groundnut
1kg (2lb 4oz) whole chicken thighs,
   legs or drumsticks
300ml (10½fl oz) chicken stock or water
2 bay leaves, scrunched a little
30g (1oz) dark (bitter) chocolate

The craft here is making the mole sauce - a process to take pleasure in. Mole means 'sauce' in Nahuatl Aztec language. I have used three different dried Mexican chillies to bring depth of heat and flavour. These different chillies are worth seeking out if you want to make good mole sauce, each bringing very different qualities. If you can source only the ancho (commonly found in bigger grocery stores), do still have a go at making the mole sauce with just the ancho chilli.

1. In a casserole pan set over a moderate heat, toast the dried chillies for around 30 seconds until aromatic. Transfer to a bowl, add the raisins or sultanas and cover with boiling water.

2. Toast the pumpkin seeds in the pan for 3 minutes, until they start to pop, then transfer to a separate bowl. Repeat with the almonds and then the sesame seeds, toasting until lightly coloured, then add to a separate bowl.

3. Turn up the heat to high to char the tomatoes, onion wedges and garlic cloves for around 5 minutes, until beginning to blacken in spots, then transfer the lot to a plate to cool slightly.

4. Drain the chillies and raisins, reserving the soaking liquid. Put the chillies, raisins, onion, tomatoes, garlic, salt, pepper, oregano, spices, almonds and sesame seeds in a food processor or blender. Add half the pumpkin seeds and blend to form a very smooth purée. You can add a splash of the soaking liquid to help with blending, if needed. This is your mole sauce.

5. Heat the oil in the casserole pan over a moderate heat. Add the chicken and brown it for around 5-10 minutes, until coloured, then remove to a plate, keeping the fat in the pan.

6. Add the mole to the pan and fry for 5 minutes over a moderate heat, stirring until thickened and just sticking to the pan.

7. Return the chicken and any of the resting juices to the pan, then add the stock or water and bay leaves. Bring to a simmer, give it a stir, then cover, reduce the heat to low, and simmer for 30-40 minutes, until the meat is tender and the sauce is thick.

8. Stir in the chocolate and check the seasoning. Remove from the heat and strew with the remaining pumpkin seeds to serve.

Chicken with Sweet Potatoes and Coconut Black Beans

Serves 4

1kg (2lb 4oz) whole chicken thighs,
    legs or drumsticks
2 tbsp olive oil
1 large onion, finely diced
1 green (bell) pepper, deseeded and
    finely diced
3 garlic cloves, finely chopped
2 bay leaves
2 thyme sprigs, leaves picked and
    finely chopped
1 tsp ground allspice
2 tsp ground cumin
2 large sweet potatoes, peeled and cut
    into 2cm (¾in) cubes
2 tbsp tomato purée (paste)
200g (7oz) canned whole plum tomatoes
1 x 400g (14oz) can of black beans,
    drained and rinsed
600ml (21fl oz) chicken stock or water
200g (7oz) coconut cream
1 small bunch of coriander (cilantro),
    leaves finely chopped
salt and freshly ground black pepper
1 juicy lime, quartered, to serve
fresh red chilli, finely sliced, to serve
    (optional)

There is an unbeatable combination of ingredients here: black beans and sweet potatoes cooked with quite a bit of allspice, thyme and cumin among others. The coconut cream really rounds off this casserole beautifully, and we haven't even mentioned the chicken yet, which is terrific, cooked as it is in the sweetly fragrant, fudgy black beans.

1. Season the chicken with salt and pepper.

2. Heat the oil in a large casserole pan over a moderate heat. Add the chicken and fry for 8-10 minutes, until golden brown. Remove to a plate, reserving the oil in the pan.

3. Add the onion and (bell) pepper and cook, stirring occasionally, for around 10 minutes, until the vegetables have softened. Add the garlic, bay, thyme and spices and cook for 1 minute more, until aromatic. Add the sweet potatoes and tomato purée (paste) and cook for 10 minutes, stirring often, or until the sweet potatoes are beginning to soften.

4. Add the plum tomatoes and black beans and simmer for 3-5 minutes, until thickened, then return the chicken to the pan, semi-burying the chicken into the beans. Add the stock or water. Bring to a simmer, and season to taste with salt and pepper. Cover with a lid and simmer for 30-40 minutes, until the chicken is cooked through and the veg is rich and thick. Stir through the coconut cream and coriander (cilantro) and warm through for around 3 minutes.

5. Check for seasoning, then divide among bowls and top with the lime wedges to squeeze and some fresh red chilli, if you like.

Chicken Adobo

80ml (2½fl oz) dark soy sauce

80ml (2¾fl oz) rice wine vinegar, or use coconut vinegar

8 garlic cloves: 4 finely chopped and 4 left whole and unpeeled

1 tsp whole black peppercorns

4 bay leaves, scrunched a little

2 tsp light brown soft sugar

1kg (2lb 4oz) whole chicken thighs, legs or drumsticks

2 tbsp vegetable or sunflower oil

1 bunch of spring onions (scallions), green and white separated and thinly sliced

freshly ground black pepper

This is a classic, family favourite Filipino dish that suits chicken and cooking in a casserole very much. The relatively short list of ingredients belies the intensity of flavour in the finished adobo. A first-rate adobo should be bracing in its acidity with a good amount of vinegar; salty with the soy and fish sauces; have a deep, numbing heat from the whole peppercorns (braised in the sauce, these then turn soft and delectably chewy); and, finally, have a faint clove-like sweetness from the bay leaves and brown sugar. The popularity of this dish in the Philippines and in communities interested in cooking the world over means there are a good many versions of adobo recipes out there – this is my version.

1. Combine the soy sauce, vinegar, finely chopped garlic, peppercorns, bay leaves and brown sugar to make a marinade.

2. Mix the marinade into the chicken, cover and marinate in the fridge for at least 1 hour, although the longer the better. Remove the chicken from the fridge about 20 minutes before you plan to cook it. Alternatively, forgo the marinating time and continue with the method below.

3. Separate the chicken from its marinade, reserving any excess marinade in the bowl.

4. Heat the oil in a casserole pan on a moderate heat. Add the chicken and fry it on both sides for about 10 minutes, until browned, then set aside on a plate, reserving the oil in the pan.

5. Add the spring onion (scallion) whites and whole garlic to the pan and fry for 5 minutes, until softened.

6. Pour in the reserved marinade and 250ml (9fl oz) of water and bring to a boil for 1 minute, then return the chicken to the pan and turn down the heat to low. Cook, uncovered, over a low heat for 8–10 minutes on one side, then turn the chicken over and gently cook for another 10–12 minutes, until cooked through, adding a splash of hot water if it dries out too much.

7. Remove the chicken from the heat and top with the spring onion greens, and plenty of freshly ground black pepper.

Chicken Paprikash

Serves 4

3 tbsp vegetable oil

2 onions, thinly sliced

2 green or red (bell) peppers, deseeded
and thinly sliced

2 garlic cloves, thinly sliced

2 bay leaves

1 tsp caraway seeds, toasted and
roughly ground

½ tsp freshly ground black pepper

2 tbsp sweet paprika, Hungarian
if possible

3 whole tomatoes (canned or fresh),
peeled and chopped

cayenne pepper, hot paprika or chilli
flakes, to taste

700g (1lb 9oz) boneless, skinless chicken
(thigh is best), diced

½ tsp salt

100g (3½oz) sour cream

I met a Hungarian opera singer a while back and, as is
common when I meet new people, it is never all that long
before the topic of food surfaces. I can happily talk about food
and cooking for hours, but I think Alinka the opera singer
could out-do me and focus for hours solely on the topic of
paprika. A symbol of Hungarian cuisine, Hungarian paprika for
the national dish of paprikash is a must. It has a sweet, unique
heat and deep, ruby-red colour. Alinka argued that Hungarian
paprika, mild to hot (you decide) and used assertively, is one
of the finest spices in all the world. Serve the paprikash with
plain rice or boiled new potatoes.

1. Heat the oil in a casserole pan over a moderate heat. Add
the onions and (bell) peppers and fry for 8–10 minutes, until
they are soft and sweet. Add the garlic and cook for another
2 minutes to soften.

2. Add the bay leaves, caraway seeds, black pepper and sweet
paprika and cook for 1 minute, then add the tomatoes and cook
for 5 more minutes, before finally adding the cayenne, hot
paprika or chilli flakes to taste.

3. Add the chicken and salt and stir to combine. Cover the pan,
reduce the heat and cook for 30–35 minutes, until the chicken
is cooked through.

4. Add the sour cream, stir to combine and remove the pan
from the heat.

40-Cloves-of-Garlic Chicken

Serves 4

1kg (2lb 4oz) whole chicken thighs,
  leg or drumsticks
2 tbsp olive oil
40 garlic cloves (approximately
  3–4 bulbs), unpeeled
250ml (9fl oz) dry white wine
2 bay leaves
1 large thyme sprig
250ml (9fl oz) chicken stock or water
salt and freshly ground black pepper

Many different food writers – from Richard Olney, Elizabeth David, Keith Floyd and Nigel Slater to Nigella Lawson, me and many more – have given the recipe for 40-cloves-of-garlic chicken (thought to be Provençale in origin), but it's terrific and it deserves its place in this book, too. The older the garlic, the more pungent the flavour, so fat cloves of new-season French garlic would no doubt be outrageously good in this recipe, but regular garlic, found already in your kitchen or in supermarket aisles, will also work perfectly well. With what seems a gargantuan number of cloves in the recipe you might expect the garlic flavour in this chicken stew to overwhelm and appeal only to die-hard garlic fans. Spoiler alert! This is a winning preparation that will, quite simply, appeal to everyone. I have used chicken legs for this recipe, making it more of a weeknight dinner. However, do have a go at braising a whole bird, if you fancy it, upping the cooking time accordingly (see the whole poached chicken recipes as reference). Some mashed, roasted or boiled potatoes would also be a good accompaniment.

1. Preheat the oven to 180°C/160°C fan/350°F/Gas 4.

2. Season the chicken with salt and pepper.

3. Heat the oil in a casserole pan over a moderate heat. Add the chicken and garlic and fry, turning, for around 8–10 minutes, until both are golden brown all over.

4. Add the wine, bay and thyme, and cook, stirring often, until the liquid is almost completely cooked away.

5. Add the stock or water and cover with a lid. Then cook over a very low heat for around 30–35 minutes, until the chicken is fully cooked through.

6. Remove the casserole pan from the heat and rest the chicken for 5 minutes before serving.

7. Eat the garlic cloves, squeezing them out from their casings, with the chicken and juices.

Chicken with Beaujolais, Prunes, Shallots and Thyme

Serves 4

1kg (2lb 4oz) whole chicken thighs,
  legs, drumsticks or breasts
50g (1¾oz) butter
4 large or 12 small shallots, peeled (leave
  the root on to help them hold together)
1 tbsp tomato purée (paste)
2 garlic cloves, finely chopped
2 thyme sprigs, plus ½ tsp picked
  thyme leaves
½ bunch flat-leaf parsley, leaves picked
  and finely chopped and stalks reserved
2 bay leaves
200ml (7fl oz) Beaujolais, or another
  young, fruity red wine
16 pitted prunes
200ml (7fl oz) chicken stock
1 tbsp Dijon, plus more to serve
salt and freshly ground black pepper

This is the ultimate autumn recipe. I'm heading to the vineyards of Burgundy to cook this, in November perhaps, when new season Gamay is washing around in abundance, eyes tight shut, work with me here…! These are all ingredients that will flatter and elevate the chicken: Beaujolais, prunes, thyme, garlic and Dijon. It's best served on a pile of buttery mashed potato, with a glass of the same wine in hand. Go old fashioned and tie your parsley and thyme stalks, wrapped in the bay leaves and secured with some kitchen string, into a bouquet garni.

1. Season the chicken with salt and pepper.

2. Melt the butter in a casserole pan over a moderate heat. Add the chicken, and fry for around 5 minutes, turning, until golden brown all over. Add the shallots and continue to cook for another 4–5 minutes, until they too have taken on a bit of colour.

3. Turn down the heat and add the tomato purée (paste), garlic, thyme sprigs, parsley stalks and bay and stir gently. Then add the wine, stirring well to dislodge any bits of caramelized chicken stuck to the pan. Simmer for a few minutes, then add the prunes and the chicken stock. Cook over a low-moderate heat for around 30–40 minutes, until the chicken is tender and cooked through.

4. Remove the chicken from the pan and leave it to rest on a plate, keeping it warm, while you reduce the liquid in the pan over a high heat for a couple of minutes to thicken it slightly. Add the Dijon and whisk to combine.

5. Add the chicken back into the sauce in the pan and season well with salt, if needed, and plenty of freshly ground black pepper. Remove from the heat and strew with the chopped parsley and picked thyme leaves, and with more mustard on the side.

Chicken with Orzo, Artichokes, Oregano and Feta

Serves 4

2 tbsp olive oil

1 red (bell) pepper, deseeded and finely diced

1 onion, finely diced

3 garlic cloves, finely chopped

2 tsp coriander seeds, roughly crushed

1 tsp dried oregano

1 tsp sweet or hot unsmoked paprika

½ tsp salt

250g (9oz) passata (strained tomatoes)

700g (1lb 9oz) boneless, skinless chicken (thigh is best), diced

300g (10½oz) orzo pasta

250ml (9fl oz) hot chicken stock or boiling water

200g (7oz) feta, crumbled

about 150g (5½oz) artichokes in oil, drained and roughly diced

½ small bunch of dill, roughly chopped

salt and freshly ground black pepper

1 lemon, quartered, to serve

I am looking to Greece for the flavours used in this one-pot. Orzo is the phantom pasta shape that likes to think it is rice. In this recipe it is cooked with tomatoes, chicken stock, plenty of cracked coriander seeds, oregano and more, then strewn all over with an unbeatable trio of feta, artichokes and parsley. Serve with some lemon wedges on the side to squeeze all over.

1. Heat the olive oil in a heavy-bottomed casserole pan over a moderate heat. Add the (bell) pepper and onion and cook for around 8-10 minutes, until soft. Add the garlic and cook for a further 1-2 minutes, until fragrant.

2. Add the coriander seeds, dried oregano, paprika and salt and stir for 1 minute, mixing briskly. Add the passata and cook for 2 minutes, then add the chicken and stir well to coat. Continue to cook over a moderate heat for about 5 more minutes.

3. Add the orzo to the pan along with the hot stock or boiling water and bring the pan to a quick simmer. Cover with a lid, reduce the heat to moderate-low and cook for about 30 minutes, until the orzo is tender and the chicken is cooked through. From time to time, give the pan a good stir as the orzo will try its best to stick to the bottom of the pan. Add a splash more water, if necessary.

4. Remove from the heat and check the seasoning of the sauce, adding plenty of freshly ground black pepper and a pinch more salt, if necessary, then strew all over with the crumbled feta, diced artichokes and chopped dill. Serve with the lemon quarters on the side.

Chicken with Borlotti Beans, Cavolo Nero and Rosemary

Serves 4

1kg (2lb 4oz) whole chicken thighs, legs or drumsticks
4 tbsp olive oil
1 large onion, finely diced
2 carrots, peeled and finely diced
2 celery stalks, finely diced
3 garlic cloves: 2 peeled and finely chopped, 1 peeled and left whole
2 tsp finely chopped rosemary leaves
¼ tsp dried chilli flakes (optional; more or less to taste)
1 x 400g (14oz) can plum tomatoes
1 large bunch (about 250g/9oz) of cavolo nero, stalks removed and finely shredded, leaves sliced into broad ribbons
800ml (28fl oz) hot chicken stock or boiling water
1 x 400g (14oz) can borlotti beans, drained and rinsed
4 slices of good crusty bread
salt and freshly ground black pepper
freshly grated parmesan, to serve

Use best-quality canned borlotti beans for this recipe. If you can't get hold of them, use an alternative such as cannellini or white beans (chickpeas would also work). I give instructions to toast some bread and rub it assertively with a raw clove of garlic and drizzle it generously with some olive oil. While, granted, this takes us beyond the maxim of One Pan Chicken, toast does not require any pan work, so my conscience is clear here.

1. Season the chicken with salt and pepper.

2. Heat 2 tablespoons of the olive oil in a large casserole pan over a moderate heat. Add the chicken and fry it for about 5 minutes on each side until golden brown all over. Remove the chicken to a plate, reserving the oil in the pan.

3. Add the onion, carrots and celery and cook, stirring occasionally, for a good 10–12 minutes, until the vegetables are soft and just starting to colour. Add the chopped garlic, rosemary leaves and chilli flakes (if using) and cook for another 2–3 minutes, until fragrant.

4. Add the tomatoes and cavolo nero stalks and leaves and cook for 10 minutes over a moderate heat until any liquid has evaporated and the mixture is nicely concentrated.

5. Return the chicken to the pan, semi-burying it into the cavolo nero. Then, add the hot stock or water. Bring the contents of the pan to a gentle simmer, season well with salt and freshly ground black pepper, pop a lid on the pan and cook over a low heat for 15–20 minutes, until the chicken is cooked through and the sauce is rich and delicious.

6. Add the beans, stirring well to combine, and warm through for 5 minutes.

7. Meanwhile toast the bread and rub each slice with the whole clove of garlic and drizzle liberally with the remaining olive oil.

8. To serve, add a piece of garlic-rubbed toast to each bowl and ladle over the chicken, cavolo nero and beans, then top each serving with plenty of freshly grated parmesan, and perhaps a final drizzle of olive oil and pinch of chilli flakes.

Chicken and Choucroute Garnie

Serves 4

1kg (2lb 4oz) whole chicken thighs,
  legs or drumsticks
2 tbsp olive oil
100g (3½oz) smoked streaky bacon,
  finely diced
30g (1oz) butter
1 large carrot, finely diced
1 large onion, finely diced
3 garlic cloves, finely diced
1 x 500g (1lb 2oz) jar of sauerkraut,
  drained
300ml (10½fl oz) chicken stock
250ml (9fl oz) white wine (ideally a
  Riesling or Pinot Gris)
2 bay leaves, scrunched a little
4 juniper berries, roughly bashed
  or squashed
2 tsp caraway seeds, roughly crushed
2 whole star anise
4 tbsp crème fraîche (optional)
salt and freshly ground black pepper
½ small bunch of flat-leaf parsley, leaves
  finely chopped, to serve
French mustard, to serve

I am rarely without a jar of sauerkraut on my shelves. I am very happy to just eat a forkful from the jar if I'm feeling hungry and in a rush. In a cheese toastie? Well, this is a given. But this being a recipe book, I am duty bound to give a lifeline to the jar of sauerkraut beyond just these two incidents, good as they both are. Enter stage left under a dazzling spotlight: choucroute garnie. It is an Alsatian dish of 'dressed sauerkraut' cooked with wine, sausages, salted meats and caraway seeds, and (because, after all, this is a book about chicken) I'm adding some chicken thighs to braise. I'm also adding a big dollop of crème fraîche at the end, enjoying the creamy depth it brings to the finished dish.

1. Season the chicken with salt and pepper.

2. Heat the oil in a casserole pan over a moderate heat. Add the chicken, skin side down, and cook for around 5 minutes, until golden brown but not yet cooked through. Flip and cook for another 5 minutes to brown on the other side, then remove to a plate, reserving the fat in the pan.

3. Add the bacon and gently sauté until crisp and very lightly coloured, around 3–5 minutes should do. Add the butter, carrot and onion and cook for around 10 minutes over a moderate–low heat, until soft and sweet. Add the garlic and cook for 2 minutes more, until fragrant. Add the sauerkraut and stir well.

4. Add the stock, wine and herbs and spices, then nestle the chicken thighs back in among the sauerkraut. Cover with a sheet of greaseproof or baking paper (cut it into a circle just larger than the pan - a cartouche, if you like) and pop a lid on the pan.

5. Braise the chicken over a moderate–low heat for 20–25 minutes, until all liquid in the pan has evaporated and the chicken is fully cooked through. Finish by checking the seasoning, adding salt and pepper to taste.

6. Stir through with the crème fraîche, if using, and strew with the parsley. Serve with mustard.

Chicken with Cider, Apples and Butter

Serves 4

1kg (2lb 4oz) whole chicken thighs, legs or drumsticks
100g (3½oz) butter, 50g (1¾oz) softened and 50g (1¾oz) chilled and diced
3 celery stalks, thinly sliced
2 onions, thinly sliced
500ml (17fl oz) dry cider
3 tart green apples, such as Granny Smith
3 cloves
1 cinnamon stick (about 10cm/4in)
1 tbsp wholegrain mustard
salt and freshly ground black pepper

I'm using half the butter to baste the chicken, with the remainder then whisked into the sauce once the chicken is cooked to emulsify the liquid into a sauce. In classical French cooking, this process is called monté – it is a completely delicious way to create a sauce, the butter rounding off the acidity in the apples and cider. With the cinnamon and cloves bringing the spice, this is a great autumn–winter casserole. Accompany with some mashed potatoes or some buttery polenta with plenty of freshly ground black pepper.

1. Preheat the oven to 180°C/160°C fan/350°F/Gas 4.

2. Smear the chicken with the softened butter. Place the celery and onions in a casserole pan, then sit the chicken on top. Season well with salt and freshly ground black pepper. Add half the cider to the pan, then cook in the oven, uncovered, for 15 minutes, until the chicken skin is nicely bronzed.

3. Meanwhile, peel, core and quarter the apples, then add the apples to the casserole pan with the remainder of the cider and the cloves and cinnamon and cook for another 10 minutes or so, with the lid on the pan, until the apples have softened and the chicken is fully cooked through.

4. Remove the chicken and apples from the casserole pan and rest them for 10 minutes somewhere warm. Bring the sauce in the pan to a simmer over a high heat and beat in the chilled butter and the mustard, mixing vigorously to amalgamate. Check the seasoning, adding more salt and freshly ground black pepper as necessary.

5. Return the chicken and apples to the pan to serve.

Chicken with Fennel, Olives and Tomatoes

Serves 4

1kg (2lb 4oz) whole chicken thighs, legs or drumsticks

3 tbsp olive oil

4 strips of unwaxed orange zest

2 bay leaves, scrunched a little

1 small bunch of flat-leaf parsley, leaves roughly chopped, with ¼ of the stalks reserved for cooking

1 tsp ground fennel seeds

1 tsp salt, plus more to season

pinch of dried chilli flakes (optional; more or less to taste)

2 onions, thinly sliced

2 large fennel bulbs, cut into 6 equal wedges

3 garlic cloves, thinly sliced

4 ripe, skinned tomatoes or 4 canned plum tomatoes (drained), roughly chopped

350ml (12fl oz) hot chicken stock or boiling water

80g (2¾oz) pitted kalamata or black olives

freshly ground black pepper

Fennel and chicken is a terrific combination. Add olives, tomatoes and parsley and you're really winning. Fennel bulb is wonderful raw in a salad, but at the other end of the scale, fennel loves to be braised until very soft and silky, its anise notes proving a great match for chicken. I like to add chilli flakes, too. I say they are optional in the recipe, but I don't really mean it in this case.

1. In a large bowl mix together the chicken, 1 tablespoon of the oil, and the orange zest, bay leaves, reserved parsley stalks, ground fennel, salt and chilli flakes (if using). Mix the chicken into the sauce and leave to marinate covered in the fridge for at least 1 hour, although the longer the better. Bring the chicken back to room temperature for 20 minutes before you cook. Alternatively, forgo the marinating time and continue with the method below.

2. Heat the remaining oil in a casserole pan over a moderate-high heat. Add the marinated chicken and cook for 5 minutes on each side, until browned all over. Place the chicken on a plate and reserve any fat back in the pan.

3. Cook the onions and fennel in the casserole pan over a moderate heat for around 10 minutes, until softened but not coloured. Add the garlic and cook for 2 minutes more, then add the tomatoes and cook for 5 minutes, until rich and thick.

4. Add the hot stock or boiling water, stir well, then add the chicken back to the pan. Reduce the heat to low and cover to simmer very gently for about 45 minutes, or until the chicken is cooked through and tender. Remove from the heat and stir though the olives. Season with salt and pepper to taste, and leave to rest for 5 minutes.

5. Scatter over the chopped parsley leaves, to serve.

Chicken Rendang

Serves 4

3 shallots, roughly chopped

2 lemongrass stalks, sliced lengthways and bruised slightly with the back of a knife or rolling pin

5 garlic cloves, roughly chopped

2 tbsp finely grated (shredded) fresh ginger

1 tsp ground cumin

1 tsp ground coriander

½–1 tsp chilli flakes, to taste

2–3 fresh bird's-eye chillies

3 tbsp vegetable oil

4 whole, dried chillies

6 makrut lime leaves

1 cinnamon stick (about 10cm/4in)

2 star anise

3 cloves

700g (1lb 9oz) boneless, skinless chicken (thigh is best), diced

1 x 400ml (14fl oz) can of coconut milk

2 tbsp seedless tamarind pulp

1 tsp salt, plus more to taste

1 tsp palm sugar or caster (superfine) sugar, plus more to taste

Rendang originates from West Sumatra in Indonesia. An extremely popular dish, it has evolved into many different versions that you'll find in the neighbouring countries of Malaysia, Singapore, Brunei and the Philippines. Having travelled in Malaysia as a chef, and eaten voraciously, intent on understanding new flavours, this recipe is my version of this Southeast Asian classic. There is a moderate list of ingredients here to source, but I can promise you, none are tricky to find and all are essential for a really good rendang.

1. Blend the shallots, ½ the lemongrass, and all the garlic, ginger, ground spices, chilli flakes and bird's-eye chillies to a smooth paste.

2. Heat the vegetable oil in a casserole pan over a low-moderate heat. Add the paste and gently fry for about 10 minutes.

3. Add the remaining lemongrass, along with the dried chillies, lime leaves and whole spices. Turn up the heat to moderate and add 100ml (3½fl oz) of cold water, bring to a simmer and gently cook until the sauce is completely dry and sticky, with all the water absorbed.

4. Add the chicken and cook gently for 10 minutes. Add the coconut milk, tamarind, salt and sugar. Simmer for 45 minutes, until you have a dark brown, rich sauce and the chicken is melting and tender. Add a spoonful of water here and there throughout the cooking process if the pan gets too dry. Check for seasoning, adding more salt or sugar to taste as you go.

5. Remove the pan from the heat and leave the rendang to rest for 5 minutes before serving.

BAKING TRAY

Sticky Sesame Marmalade Chicken Wings

Serves 4

1 tsp salt, plus more to season
½ tsp ground star anise or ground fennel
   seeds, plus 2 whole star anise
3 garlic cloves, finely chopped
1 tbsp finely grated (shredded)
   fresh ginger
2 tbsp marmalade
2 tbsp vegetable oil
2 tsp dark soy sauce
juice from 1 lime
juice from 1 small orange (use Seville
   orange if in season)
2 tbsp sesame seeds
1kg (2lb 4oz) chicken wings (or use
   drumsticks)
ground black pepper

A great big pile of sticky-with-marmalade and freckled-with-sesame-seeds chicken wings. I must warn you now that you will need to arm yourselves with an even bigger pile of paper napkins and begin what will inevitably be one of the messiest mealtimes around. Cue much chin dabbing, finger licking, and, no doubt, an almighty scramble for the last wing, so swift will be their demolition.

1. Combine the salt and ground star anise or fennel seeds in a large bowl with the garlic, ginger, marmalade, oil, soy sauce, citrus juices, whole star anise and half the sesame seeds. Season with plenty of coarsely ground black pepper.

2. Add the chicken and mix it through to coat it all over. Cover and leave the chicken to marinate in the fridge for at least 1 hour, although the longer the better. Remove the chicken from the fridge about 20 minutes before you plan to cook it. Alternatively, forgo the marinating time and continue with the method below.

3. Preheat the oven to 200°C/180°C fan/400°F/Gas 6.

4. Place the chicken on a baking tray lined with greaseproof paper (this will help when it comes to the washing up).

5. Bake the chicken for about 35 minutes, turning the wings a few times to glaze and baste in the sauce.

6. Sprinkle the chicken pieces all over with the remaining sesame seeds, then cook for a further 10 minutes, until the chicken is well cooked through.

7. Remove from the oven and serve.

Lemongrass, Lime Leaf and Ginger Chicken

Serves 4

4 garlic cloves, roughly chopped
1 small shallot or ½ small red onion, roughly chopped
1 lemongrass stalk, roughly chopped
juice of 1 lime
1 tbsp grated (shredded) fresh ginger
1 tbsp light brown soft sugar
3 tbsp fish sauce (or use soy sauce)
½ tsp coarsely cracked black pepper (though white pepper would be entirely appropriate)
½–1 tsp chilli flakes, to taste
10 makrut lime leaves: 5 thinly shredded, 5 whole
1kg (2lb 4oz) whole chicken thighs, legs or drumsticks

For the salad
juice of 1 lime
1 tbsp fish sauce
1 tsp light brown soft sugar
3 tbsp cold water
1 garlic clove, crushed
½ small head pointed cabbage, very finely sliced
1 carrot, peeled and coarsely grated
1 small bunch of coriander (cilantro), leaves roughly chopped
1 small bunch of mint, leaves roughly chopped
3 tbsp crispy fried onions

Chicken baked with makrut lime leaves, lemongrass, ginger and lime, this recipe is very good indeed. I've also given an incredibly quick salad to make to accompany alongside. It doesn't use another pan (those are the rules), but you will need a mixing bowl to assemble it. Wow, is it worth it?!

1. Place all the chicken ingredients (minus the chicken itself and the whole lime leaves) into a blender or food processor and blitz to a coarse paste. Stir in the whole lime leaves.

2. Tip the chicken and the marinade into a large bowl and mix them together. Leave to marinate covered in the fridge for at least 1 hour, although the longer the better. Remove the chicken from the fridge about 20 minutes before you plan to cook it. Alternatively, forgo the marinating time and continue with the method below.

3. Preheat the oven to 220°C/200°C fan/425°F/Gas 7.

4. Place the chicken on a baking tray and roast for about 35–40 minutes, turning the chicken pieces in the juices a few times during roasting to glaze and baste, until the skin is richly browned and crisp and the chicken is cooked through. Remove from the oven and set aside to rest while you assemble the salad.

5. Toss all the ingredients for the vibrant, crunchy salad together in a large bowl, reserving a few crispy fried onions to sprinkle on top, then serve the cooked chicken alongside.

Sweet-and-Sour Sicilian-style Chicken

Serves 4

1 large red onion, finely diced

1 large aubergine (eggplant), finely diced

2 large potatoes, peeled and finely diced

1 red or yellow (bell) pepper, deseeded
  and diced

3 tbsp olive oil, plus a splash more
  to serve

1kg (2lb 4oz) whole chicken thighs,
  legs or drumsticks

20 cherry tomatoes, halved

juice of 1 orange (blood orange would
  be fantastic)

2 garlic cloves, finely chopped

40g (1½oz) raisins

3 tbsp red wine vinegar, plus a splash
  more to serve

30g (1oz) black olives, pitted and
  roughly chopped

1 small bunch of flat-leaf parsley,
  leaves roughly chopped

½ tsp chilli flakes (optional)

salt and freshly ground black pepper

My absolute favourite kind of cooking here – big, bold, juicy flavours. I developed this recipe specifically with Sicily in mind – it's perfect for the high heat of late summer with ripe tomatoes, peppers and aubergines all cooked to a soft slump, bright with a splash of red wine vinegar, salty with inky black olives and sweet with a handful of raisins.

1. Preheat the oven to 200°C/180°C fan/400°F/Gas 6.

2. Mix the onion, aubergine (eggplant), potatoes and (bell) peppers with the olive oil and season with salt and pepper. Tip into a baking tray and roast for 10 minutes, stirring once or twice throughout, until very softened.

3. Season the chicken with salt and pepper, and place the pieces on top of the vegetables, along with the tomatoes, orange juice and garlic and return to the oven to cook for 35–40 minutes, stirring the chicken pieces back into the juices a few times to glaze and baste, until the chicken is golden and cooked through.

4. While the chicken is cooking, soak the raisins in the vinegar.

5. With the chicken cooked and the vegetables all soft, remove the tray from the oven and stir through the raisins (with their soaking vinegar), olives and parsley.

6. Add the chilli flakes, if using, then check the seasoning, adding more salt and pepper to taste. Drizzle everything with a little more olive oil and a final splash of vinegar, if you think it needs it, then serve.

Chicken Braciole

Serves 4

4 large boneless skinless chicken breasts,
   sliced in half horizontally
8 slices of prosciutto
200g (7oz) cherry tomatoes, halved
salt and freshly ground black pepper

For the filing
50g (1¾oz) fresh breadcrumbs
2 tbsp toasted pine nuts, plus more
   to scatter
2 tbsp raisins, soaked in warm water for
   5 minutes then drained
50g (1¾oz) parmesan, finely grated
50g (1¾oz) pecorino, finely grated
   (or provolone - the traditional choice)
1 egg, beaten
¼ small bunch of flat-leaf parsley,
   leaves finely chopped
¼ small bunch of basil, leaves finely
   chopped
1 tbsp chopped rosemary or thyme leaves
zest of 1 unwaxed lemon, then that same
   lemon quartered, to serve
1 garlic clove, very finely chopped
   or crushed

You will also need
cocktail sticks, small skewers or
   kitchen string

Braciole is Italian-American in origin, and if you have watched
and enjoyed the runaway success that was *The Bear* on TV
(a programme about a young chef running a restaurant
in Chicago), you might want to have a go at making it. It's
usually made with beef or veal, but I'm using chicken breast,
which suits the dish very well.

1. Using a rolling pin, gently flatten the chicken pieces between
two sheets of baking paper until each is approximately 1.5–2cm
(⅝–¾in) thick. Season well all over with salt and freshly ground
black pepper.

2. Preheat the oven to 230°C/210°C fan/450°F/Gas 8.

3. Mix all the filling ingredients together and divide the mixture
into 8 equal portions.

4. Lay out a slice of prosciutto, top with a piece of chicken, then
spoon one portion of the filling on top of the chicken. Roll it
up tight, securing it with 2 cocktail sticks or small skewers or
string. Repeat with the rest of the chicken.

5. Arrange the tomatoes and chicken on a baking tray and
roast for around 35–40 minutes, until the chicken is crisp and
golden brown and is cooked through. Roughly 3 minutes before
the end of the cooking time, scatter the extra pine nuts in the
tray to toast.

6. Allow to rest for 5 minutes then serve whole or sliced,
spooning some of the tomatoes and their juices on to each plate,
with a lemon wedge on the side for squeezing over.

Chimichurri Chicken with Roast Squash

Serves 4

1kg (2lb 4oz) whole chicken thighs,
   legs or drumsticks
800g (1lb 12oz) squash, peeled,
   deseeded and very thinly sliced
2 red onions, thinly sliced
3 tbsp olive oil
2 tsp thyme leaves
salt and freshly ground black pepper

For the chimichurri
(or use about 120g/ 1¾oz store-bought)
1 garlic clove, finely chopped
1 tsp dried oregano
2 tbsp white wine or cider vinegar,
   plus more if needed
juice of ½ lemon
½ tsp chilli flakes
1 small bunch of flat-leaf parsley
1 shallot, finely chopped
70ml (2¼fl oz) olive oil, plus more
   if needed

Chimichurri is a pungent green Argentinian sauce made using fresh herbs, vinegar and garlic. In this recipe, I've used half the chimichurri to marinate the chicken, and I've served the remainder as the accompanying sauce. This way you get double whammy flavour on the chicken – deep and flavoursome to cook, fresh and vibrant to serve. Roasting the squash at the same time as the chicken on the tray is a tremendous match for both chicken and chimichurri and a popular vegetable (fruit!) for asado-style cooking in Argentina.

1. Blend together all of the ingredients for the chimichurri until smooth, adding salt, plus more vinegar to taste and more oil to loosen, if required.

2. Mix half the chimichurri into the chicken, cover and leave to marinate in the fridge for at least 1 hour, although the longer the better. Remove the chicken from the fridge about 20 minutes before you plan to cook it. Alternatively, forgo the marinating time and continue with the method below.

3. Preheat the oven to 200°C/180°C fan/400°F/Gas 6.

4. In a large baking tray, combine the squash and onions with 2 tablespoons of the olive oil and all the thyme leaves, then season with salt and pepper. Place the chicken on top and drizzle with the remaining tablespoon of olive oil and again season with salt and pepper.

5. Roast for about 35–40 minutes, or until the chicken is completely cooked and tender. Add more seasoning if needed, then drizzle with the remaining chimichurri to serve.

Elote-style Chicken with Corn

Serves 4

2-4 tbsp chipotle paste, to taste; plus more to serve if you like it extra-hot
4 garlic cloves, crushed
2 tbsp vegetable or olive oil
1kg (2lb 4oz) whole chicken thighs, legs or drumsticks
100g (3½oz) mayonnaise
200g (7oz) feta, crumbled (or use Cotija and Chihuahua cheese, grated/shredded, if you can get it)
4 corn on the cobs, halved
½ small bunch of coriander (cilantro), leaves roughly chopped
30g (1oz) fried maize (kikos), crushed to a coarse powder
2 limes, cut into wedges
salt and freshly ground black pepper

I've long been a fan of sweetcorn served elote style – the Mexican street-food preparation of sweetcorn grilled then basted with a highly seasoned mayonnaise and dusted with a mountain of freshly grated cheese, with lime and chilli of choice to serve. It is quite simply, the best way to eat sweetcorn – no ifs, no buts. This got me thinking – adding chicken turns this into a full meal and is an absolute must.

1. Mix half the chipotle paste and all the garlic with the oil.

2. Mix this into the chicken, cover and leave to marinate in the fridge for at least 1 hour, although the longer the better. Remove the chicken from the fridge about 20 minutes before you plan to cook it. Alternatively, forgo the marinating time and continue with the method below.

3. Mix the remaining chipotle into the mayonnaise along with half the crumbled or grated cheese.

4. Preheat the oven to 220°C/200°C fan/425°F/Gas 7.

5. Season the marinated chicken and the corn well with salt and plenty of freshly ground black pepper and arrange in a baking tray. Roast for 40-45 minutes, until the chicken is golden brown and cooked through and the corn tender and with some colour.

6. Dollop the mayonnaise mixture all over the corn and chicken, along with a bit more chipotle paste if you like, then sprinkle with the remaining cheese and strew with the coriander (cilantro) and fried maize.

7. Serve with lime wedges on the side for squeezing over.

Chicken with Grainy Mustard, Honey and Orange

Serves 4

2 tbsp grainy mustard
1 tbsp red wine vinegar
3 garlic cloves, finely chopped
2 tsp runny honey
2 tbsp vegetable oil
juice from 1 large orange, or the juice
    from 2 Seville oranges if in season
1kg (2lb 4oz) whole chicken thighs,
    legs or drumsticks
1 tsp salt, plus more to season
4 bay leaves
2 red onions, thinly sliced into rounds
freshly ground black pepper

I'm a big fan of using grainy mustard in a marinade. Here the mustard is slackened with some orange juice and red wine vinegar and given a bit of sweetness from a drizzle of honey. When Seville oranges are in season, use their juice – I find the bright and bitter Seville orange juice delicious in all kinds of winter cooking, not just for marmalade.

1. Combine the mustard, vinegar, garlic, honey, oil and orange juice in a large bowl.

2. Add the chicken, mix, cover and leave marinate in the fridge for at least 1 hour, although the longer the better. Remove the chicken from the fridge about 20 minutes before you plan to cook it. Alternatively, forgo the marinating time and continue with the method below.

3. Preheat the oven to 200°C/180°C fan/400°F/Gas 6.

4. Season the chicken all over with the 1 teaspoon of salt and plenty of freshly ground black pepper. Arrange the bay leaves and onions in the base of the baking tray and put the seasoned chicken on top.

5. Bake for about 45 minutes, spooning the juices over the chicken pieces a few times to glaze and baste them, until the chicken is cooked through.

6. Remove the tray from the oven and leave the chicken to rest for 5 minutes before serving with the onions and any of the syrupy pan juices.

Miso Mustard Butter Chicken and Sweetheart Cabbage

Serves 4

1 tbsp Dijon mustard
120g (1¼oz) butter, softened at
   room temperature
3 garlic cloves, crushed to a paste
   with a little salt
3 tbsp white miso
2 small pointed, sweetheart or hispi
   cabbages, trimmed and halved
2 tbsp olive oil
2 tbsp cider or white wine vinegar
1kg (2lb 4oz) whole chicken thighs,
   legs or drumsticks
50g (1¾oz) walnuts or hazelnuts,
   roughly chopped
1 small bunch of flat-leaf parsley,
   thinly sliced
salt and freshly ground black pepper

The assembly of this dish couldn't really be any easier, and if you think baked chicken and cabbage sounds, well, a bit pedestrian, this is definitely not the case. Try to source a pointed, sweetheart or hispi cabbage for this recipe – the loose structure of the leaves means they suit roasting very well. Softened butter mixed through with miso and mustard is a tremendous combination, used in this recipe to season and baste the chicken and cabbage as it melts in the oven. Be sure to scoop up all the pan juices when you come to serve the chicken.

1. Beat the mustard, butter, garlic and miso together and put the mixture to one side.

2. Preheat the oven to 220°C/200°C fan/425°F/Gas 7.

3. Rub the cabbages lightly with the olive oil and vinegar and season generously with salt, ensuring that all sides are well coated. Arrange them on a baking tray. Season the chicken pieces with salt and pepper and nestle these around the cabbage.

4. Bake the chicken and cabbage for 15 minutes, then remove the tray from the oven and dot the chicken and cabbage all over with the miso and mustard butter. Return to the oven for 15-20 minutes. Next add the walnuts or hazelnuts to the tray and cook for a further 5 minutes, until the chicken is cooked through and the cabbage is soft and slightly charred.

5. Remove from the oven, baste the cabbage and chicken with the juices in the base of the pan, then strew all over with the chopped parsley and plenty more ground black pepper.

Chicken with Peanuts, Chilli and Coconut

Serves 4

4 garlic cloves, sliced

2 tbsp light brown soft sugar
  (or use honey)

4 tbsp dark soy sauce

1 tsp ground turmeric

2 tsp ground coriander

1–2 tsp chilli flakes, to taste

1 lemongrass stalk, outer layers removed,
  root trimmed, and stem thinly sliced

2 tbsp vegetable or groundnut oil

200ml (7fl oz) full-fat coconut milk

1kg (2lb 4oz) whole chicken thighs,
  legs or drumsticks

250g (9oz) roasted peanuts (skin on or
  off, as you like)

2 limes: 1 juiced, 1 cut into wedges
  to serve

2 bunches of spring onions (scallions),
  trimmed and cut into 4cm (1½in)
  lengths

2 red chillies, thinly sliced (deseeded if
  you want less heat)

1 small bunch of coriander (cilantro),
  leaves roughly chopped

For this recipe, I am looking at Satay Chicken for inspiration. Satay is the national dish of Indonesia and Malaysia, but it can also be found in restaurants and kitchens elsewhere in much of Southeast Asia, too. In the spirit of this chapter, I've used whole chicken pieces to marinate then roast on a tray for swift ease, rather than threading the meat onto small skewers to grill over hot coals. For these reasons, this is not a satay recipe but a chicken dish cooked very much with satay flavours in mind.

1. Blend the garlic, half the sugar and half the soy sauce together with ground spices, chilli flakes, lemongrass, oil and 100ml (3½fl oz) of the coconut milk, to form a smooth paste.

2. Mix the coconut-milk mixture with the chicken, cover and leave to marinate in the fridge for at least 1 hour, although the longer the better. Remove the chicken from the fridge about 20 minutes before you plan to cook it. Alternatively, forgo the marinating time and continue with the method below.

3. Blend half the peanuts together with the remaining sugar, soy sauce and coconut milk and the lime juice, and put to one side.

4. Preheat the oven to 220°C/200°C fan/425°F/Gas 7.

5. Arrange the chicken and any excess marinade in a baking tray along with the spring onions (scallions).

6. Bake for 35–40 minutes, until the chicken is golden, beginning to char and cooked through.

7. Remove from the oven and drizzle with the coconut–peanut sauce, then sprinkle with the remaining peanuts and the fresh chilli and chopped coriander (cilantro).

8. Serve with the lime wedges on the side for squeezing over.

Za'atar Chicken served with Hummus, Pine Nuts and Pomegranate

Serves 4

700g (1lb 9oz) boneless skinless chicken
  pieces (thigh is best), diced
2 tbsp olive oil
2 tsp ground cumin
2 tsp ground coriander
2 garlic cloves, crushed with ½ tsp salt
3 tbsp za'atar
2 tbsp pomegranate molasses
3 tbsp pine nuts (or roughly chopped
  pistachios)
1 small pomegranate, deseeded
1 small bunch of coriander (cilantro) or
  flat-leaf parsley, leaves roughly chopped

For the hummus
(or use about 400g/14oz store-bought)
1 x 400g (14oz) can of chickpeas
  (garbanzos), drained
juice of ½ lemon
1 garlic clove
1 generous tbsp tahini
4 tbsp good olive oil
salt and freshly ground black pepper

Za'atar is a Middle Eastern blend of dried thyme (the herb itself is also known as za'atar in Arabic), sumac, salt and sesame seeds and can be used as a finishing condiment in many different dishes, from eggs to soups to flat breads and grilled meat and fish. It is delicious and indispensable to your storecupboard, to be bought little and often for tip-top condition. You can make your own – there are plenty of recipes online, but you can also buy ready-made blends in most larger supermarkets. I've given the recipe for hummus (which takes us beyond the one-pan ethos, I know) – by all means buy some ready-made or just turn a blind eye to a little extra washing up just this once.

1. First, make the hummus (if making homemade). Put half the chickpeas (garbanzos) with 4 tablespoons of water and all the remaining hummus ingredients, apart from the olive oil, into a blender and blitz to form a thick, smooth paste. Once smooth, add the olive oil and blend until emulsified. Season well with salt to taste. Keep to one side.

2. Mix the chicken with the olive oil, cumin, coriander and garlic. Add half the za'atar and half the pomegranate molasses.

3. Preheat the oven to 220°C/200°C fan/425°F/Gas 7.

4. Tip the chicken and the remaining chickpeas (garbanzos) into a baking tray and bake for 15–20 minutes, turning the chicken pieces over halfway through, until the chicken is cooked. Roughly 3 minutes before the end of the cooking time, add the pine nuts (or pistachios) to the tray to toast.

5. Spread out the hummus on to a large serving platter (or individual plates), top with the cooked chicken and chickpeas and spoon over any of the cooking juices.

6. Drizzle the remaining molasses and sprinkle the remaining za'atar over the dish, then scatter with the pomegranate seeds and chopped coriander (cilantro) or parsley.

Piri-Piri Chicken

Serves 4

4–6 red bird's-eye chillies, chopped
  (deseeded if you want less heat),
  to taste
6 garlic cloves, peeled
1 tsp dried oregano
2 tsp smoked paprika
3 tbsp olive or groundnut oil
3 tbsp red or white wine vinegar
juice of 1 large lemon
1kg (2lb 4oz) whole chicken thighs,
  legs, drumsticks or wings
salt and freshly ground black pepper

Piri-piri or peri-peri is the name used in Portuguese and a number of African languages to describe the diminutive African bird's-eye chilli. There are a vast number of recipes for this chicken dish, using specifically these chillies, but if all the Portuguese and African iterations have one commonality it's that the chicken should have a fiery hot, direct heat that only bird's-eye chillies can bring.

1. Blend the chillies, garlic, oregano, paprika, oil, vinegar and lemon juice to form a smooth sauce, add plenty of freshly ground black pepper and a big, big pinch of salt to taste.

2. Mix half the sauce into the chicken, cover and leave to marinate in the fridge for at least 1 hour, although the longer the better. Remove the chicken from the fridge about 20 minutes before you plan to cook it. Alternatively, forgo the marinating time and continue with the method below.

3. Preheat the oven to 220°C/200°C fan/425°F/Gas 7.

4. Line a baking tray with some foil and top with a wire rack. Arrange the chicken pieces in a single layer on the rack.

5. Bake the chicken for about 25–35 minutes for the wings, drumsticks or small thighs or 35–45 minutes for large thighs or legs, until cooked through and the skin is crisp with good colour. During the cooking time, baste the chicken with the cooking juices a couple of times, spooning the sauce and cooking juices in the pan back over the chicken as it cooks.

6. Remove from the oven and rest for 5 minutes before serving along with any remaining sauce on the side.

Chicken with Ratatouille

Serves 4

500g (1lb 2oz) cherry tomatoes
2 tsp thyme leaves
5 garlic cloves, sliced
100ml (3½fl oz) olive oil
1 large aubergine (eggplant), cut into
about 2cm (¾in) dice
2 courgettes (zucchini), cut into
about 2cm (¾in) dice
2 red (bell) peppers, deseeded and cut
into about 2cm (¾in) dice
1kg (2lb 4oz) whole chicken thighs,
legs, drumsticks or breasts
2 onions, thinly sliced
salt and freshly ground black pepper

Summer in France is the inspiration behind this recipe: lots of thyme and garlic cooked with the unbeatable mix of aubergines, peppers, courgettes and tomatoes. I am of the school of thought that on no occasion must ratatouille ever be served piping hot – just warm or at room temperature for the flavours to meld and for everything to sprawl into a fantastically delicious-tasting stew. Add roast chicken and all will be well with the world.

1. Preheat the oven to 200°C/180°C fan/400°F/Gas 6.

2. In a large baking tray or roasting tin, combine the tomatoes, thyme and garlic with 2 tablespoons of the olive oil. Season well with salt and pepper. Roast for 15–20 minutes, until the tomatoes are collapsed and juicy, then spoon this mixture to one side in a wide serving dish.

3. In the same baking tray or roasting tin, combine the aubergine (eggplant), courgettes (zucchini) and (bell) peppers together with a big pinch of salt and 40ml (1¼fl oz) of the remaining olive oil and roast for about 25 minutes, turning all the vegetables halfway through the cook time, until they are tender and cooked but still with form and not too mushy. Add the baked vegetables to the cooked tomatoes and keep to one side somewhere warm.

4. Use the same tin now to cook the chicken. Combine the chicken, onions and remaining olive oil in the roasting tin and season this well with salt and plenty of pepper. Roast for about 35–40 minutes, until the chicken is cooked through and tender.

5. Remove from the oven and place the chicken on top of the ratatouille. Rest for about 5 minutes before serving.

ROASTING TIN

Whole Roast Chicken with Lemon, Garlic, Fennel and Bay

Serves 4

3 good thyme sprigs, leaves picked
    from 2 sprigs, 1 kept whole
finely grated zest of 1 unwaxed lemon,
    that same lemon then halved for
    squeezing
2 garlic cloves, finely crushed
2 tsp fennel seeds, bashed a little
40g (1½oz) butter, softened at room
    temperature, or 3 tbsp olive oil
1 whole chicken (about 1.5kg/3lb 5oz)
1 onion, cut into 1cm (½in) slices
1 fennel bulb, trimmed and cut
    into 1cm (½in) slices
3 bay leaves, scrunched a little
chicken stock or water
salt and freshly ground black pepper

If there is one simple version of whole roast chicken that I cook most often and without all that much forethought or preparation, it is probably this. With Italy in mind, the chicken is cooked with lemons, fennel and garlic – some indecently crisp roasted potatoes and a pile of simply cooked seasonal greens with lemon and olive oil alongside would be perfect. I think I was probably aged around 11 years old when my mum first taught me to roast a whole chicken. Roasting a chicken well is a lifelong skill that will feed you, your family and many friends for years to come. The riffs from here are endless, just master this simple technique to begin with. At the very least you must ensure your chicken is well-seasoned and never, ever let the roasting tin dry out and scorch – there lies a spoilt dinner.

1. Preheat the oven to 220°C/200°C fan/425°F/Gas 7.

2. Mix the picked thyme leaves, lemon zest, garlic and fennel seeds into the butter or oil. Rub the chicken all over with the flavoured butter or oil, pushing some of the butter or oil up and under or between the flesh and skin; just take care not to tear the skin. Season generously, both inside and out, with salt and black pepper.

3. Place the onion and fennel slices in a roasting tin, then place the chicken on top. Add the bay leaves and whole thyme sprig to the cavity of the chicken.

4. Add 1cm (½in) depth of chicken stock or water to the bottom of the tin and roast for 1 hour–1 hour 20 minutes, until golden brown and the juices run clear when you push a skewer into the largest and juiciest part of the chicken leg. You can also test by using a digital thermometer until it gives an internal meat temperature of 75°C/167°F. Adding a splash more water or stock to the pan throughout the cooking time is paramount to stop the pan and chicken from scorching in a dry pan.

5. Allow the chicken to rest for 20 minutes before carving, straining any cooking juices to serve, and squeezing over the lemon juice.

Whole Roast Cinnamon Chicken with Rice

Serves 4

250g (9oz) basmati rice
1 whole chicken (about 1.5kg/3lb 5oz)
4 tbsp olive oil
1 tsp salt, plus more to season
3 tsp ground cinnamon
4 bay leaves
2 onions, thinly sliced
1 tsp ground cardamom
1 tsp ground allspice
500ml (17fl oz) hot chicken stock
  (or use boiling water)
1 cinnamon stick (about 10cm/4in)
salt and freshly ground black pepper
lemon wedges, to serve

This recipe featured in my very first book, *The 5 O'Clock Apron*. Ten years on and eight cookbooks later, this is still very much a favourite for my whole family. The whole chicken cooks over the rice, with the spices scenting both the chicken and the rice to create the most deliciously sticky chicken pilaf, a perfect accompaniment to the roast chicken itself. My friend Jemma gave me the bare bones to this recipe, the origins of which were given to her by her Jewish grandmother, herself apparently a very fine cook.

1. Preheat the oven to 220°C/200°C fan/425°F/Gas 7.

2. Rinse the rice in plenty of cold running water, then drain well and set aside.

3. Rub the chicken all over with the oil, salt and half the ground cinnamon. Put the bay leaves and a big pinch of salt into the chicken cavity.

4. Place the onions into a deep roasting tin and add 1cm (½in) depth of water. Place the chicken breast-side up on top. Roast for 30 minutes, until coloured.

5. Remove the pan from the oven and place the par-cooked chicken on a large plate.

6. Add the well-drained rice to the onion mixture along with the remaining ground spices and stir well to coat, then pour over the hot stock and season with salt. Place the whole cinnamon stick inside the chicken.

7. Place the par-cooked chicken back in the middle of the tin, on top of the rice, cover tightly with foil and return to the oven to cook for about 30–40 minutes, until the chicken and rice are cooked and the liquid is absorbed.

8. Remove from the heat and allow the dish to rest, covered, for 15 minutes.

9. Give the rice and chicken a final seasoning with salt and a generous grinding of fresh black pepper, then serve with wedges of lemon to squeeze over at the table.

Spatchcocked Chicken with Yogurt, Harissa and Preserved Lemon

Serves 4

50g (1¾oz) harissa
100g (3½oz) plain yogurt
½ tsp freshly ground black pepper, plus more to season
1 tsp salt, plus more to season
1 whole chicken (about 1.5kg/3lb 5oz), spatchcocked (ask your butcher to do this for you if you prefer)
1 large onion, thinly sliced
2 small, preserved lemons, seeds removed, flesh and skin very finely chopped
80g (2¾oz) green olives, pitted and finely chopped
a small bunch of coriander (cilantro), leaves roughly chopped

A butcher will easily be able to spatchcock a chicken for you, and some supermarkets sell chickens spatchcocked. If you're up for the challenge, though, there are also plenty of good souls online who will be able to show you how to do it. This is a failsafe recipe: few ingredients, cooked well, for a crowd-pleasing centrepiece. Serve with your favourite side dishes; this is one to cook and take along to a summer picnic or barbecue.

1. Mix the harissa with the yogurt, the ½ teaspoon of ground black pepper and the teaspoon of salt to form a smooth sauce.

2. Mix the chicken into the sauce, cover and leave to marinate in the fridge for at least 1 hour, although the longer the better. Remove the chicken from the fridge about 20 minutes before you plan to cook it. Alternatively, forgo the marinating time and continue with the method below.

3. Preheat the oven to 200°C/180°C fan/400°F/Gas 6.

4. Place the onion in a deep roasting tin and pop the chicken on top, then add 1cm (½in) water.

5. Roast the chicken for about 35–45 minutes, or until cooked through with good colour and beginning to char around the edges.

6. Remove from the oven and allow to rest for 10 minutes before serving strewn all over with the chopped preserved lemon, green olives and coriander (cilantro) leaves.

Chicken Dauphinoise with Dijon and Cream

Serves 4

250ml (9fl oz) double (heavy) cream
150ml (5fl oz) whole milk
2 garlic cloves, crushed
1 tsp thyme leaves
1 tbsp Dijon mustard
2 bay leaves, scrunched a little
1 nutmeg, a good grating (or a pinch
  of ground)
50g (1¾oz) parmesan, finely grated
800g (1lb 12oz) small waxy potatoes,
  very thinly sliced (skin on)
1kg (2lb 4oz) whole chicken thighs,
  legs or drumsticks
butter, for dotting, if necessary
salt and freshly ground black pepper

Looks fancy this recipe, although it is really very easy to make. Ideally, use a mandoline to slice the potatoes - a sharp piece of kitchen equipment, a mandoline is inexpensive and easy to come by, and incredibly useful for slicing potatoes or other ingredients in an exacting fashion. This means that the potatoes then all cook perfectly in unison. For this recipe the potatoes are partially submerged in a Dijon mustard-laced cream, with the tops of the potatoes protruding to fan and blister in the heat of the oven, the chicken pieces snug, nicely nestled in the cream and potatoes to cook at the same time.

1. Preheat the oven to 200°C/180°C fan/400°F/Gas 6.

2. Mix the cream and milk along with the garlic, thyme, mustard, bay, nutmeg and plenty of black pepper in a large bowl, then add salt to taste. Stir through half the parmesan, then add the potatoes and chicken and stir to coat everything in the cream. Remove the chicken to a plate.

3. Arrange the creamy potatoes in a roasting tin or baking dish, fanning them out, then nestle the chicken in, skin-side up.

4. Cover the roasting tin with a lid or foil and bake the chicken and potatoes for 30–40 minutes. Remove the foil, sprinkle the remaining parmesan on top and bake for a further 30 minutes, until browned on top and cooked through. If you feel the potatoes and chicken skin need more colour, you can dot them with butter and pop the dish under a hot grill (broiler) for 5 minutes.

5. Remove from the oven and allow the dish to rest for 5 minutes before serving.

Spatchcocked Chicken with Yogurt, Almonds, Saffron, Cardamom and Rosewater

Serves 4

½ tsp ground green cardamom

2 tsp garam masala

50g (1¾oz) ground almonds

2 garlic cloves, crushed

1 tbsp finely grated (shredded)
    fresh ginger

1 tsp rosewater (not essence)

big pinch of caster (superfine) sugar

100g (3½oz) plain yogurt

good pinch of saffron, soaked in 1 tbsp
    warm water

juice of 1 lemon

1 tsp salt, plus more to season

1 whole chicken (about 1.5kg/3lb 5oz),
    spatchcocked (ask your butcher to do
    this for you if you prefer)

1 large onion, thinly sliced

40g (1½oz) flaked almonds

40g (1½oz) raisins

½ small bunch of mint, leaves
    roughly chopped

salt and freshly ground black pepper

Serendipity is the bottle of rosewater in the cupboard. I hope you'll believe me when I say that there are many people (from where I write this book, here in the UK) with a bottle of rosewater on their shelves and not a clue what to do with it, or why they first purchased it. Rosewater is used a lot in Iranian, Arabic and Indian cooking, mostly to give a delicate rose aroma to many different sweets and desserts. It is also used in some savoury cooking, sparingly, to impart an elusive can't-quite-put-your-finger-on-it aroma to a cooked dish. In this chicken recipe, combined with almonds, cardamom, saffron and garam masala, it is mouthwatering.

1. Mix the ground spices, ground almonds, garlic, ginger, rosewater and sugar with the yogurt, saffron (with the soaking water), half the lemon juice and the 1 teaspoon of salt to form a smooth sauce.

2. Mix the chicken into the sauce, cover and leave to marinate in the fridge for at least 1 hour, although the longer the better. Remove the chicken from the fridge about 20 minutes before you plan to cook it. Alternatively, forgo the marinating time and continue with the method below.

3. Preheat the oven to 200°C/180°C fan/400°F/Gas 6.

4. Place the onion in a deep roasting tin and place the chicken on top, then add 1cm (½in) depth of water.

5. Roast the chicken for 30–40 minutes, then add the flaked almonds to toast on top of the chicken. Cook for a further 5 minutes, until the chicken is cooked through with good colour and beginning to char around the edges. Remove from the oven and squeeze over the remaining lemon juice.

6. Allow to rest for 10 minutes, then serve topped with the raisins and mint.

Whole Roast Chicken with Porcini and Truffle Stuffing

Serves 4

3 garlic cloves, crushed

2 tsp thyme leaves

80g (2¾oz) butter, melted

20g (¾oz) dried porcini mushrooms, rinsed and soaked in 100ml (3½fl oz) boiling water

bunch of spring onions (scallions), trimmed, white parts very thinly sliced, green parts reserved for another use

110g (3¾oz) fresh white breadcrumbs

1 tbsp truffle oil or truffle paste

1 small bunch of flat-leaf parsley, leaves finely chopped

1 whole chicken (about 1.5kg/3lb 5oz)

1 onion, sliced into 2cm (¾in) rings

dry white wine, chicken stock or water

salt and freshly ground black pepper

Porcini and truffle mixed through with spring onions, garlic and breadcrumbs - all here as a stuffing, the flavours swelling as the chicken roasts, creating a mouthwatering combination. Why not serve this roast chicken with some roast potatoes and a great big pile of buttery cooked greens?

1. Preheat the oven to 200°C/180°C fan/400°F/Gas 6.

2. Mix half the garlic and half the thyme leaves into half the melted butter.

3. Drain the porcini (reserving the liquid) and finely chop them.

4. Mix the finely sliced white parts of the spring onions (scallions) together with the mushrooms into the garlic butter, then add the breadcrumbs, truffle oil or paste and parsley. Season well with salt and pepper and mix well. Use this to stuff inside the cavity of the chicken.

5. Mix the remaining thyme leaves and garlic into the remaining butter.

6. Rub the chicken all over with the flavoured butter, pushing some of the butter up and under or between the flesh and skin, just take care not to tear the skin. Season the chicken generously with salt and pepper.

7. Place the onion in a deep roasting tin, then place the chicken on top. Add the mushroom soaking liquid to the tin.

8. Add a 1cm (½in) depth of dry white wine, chicken stock or water to the bottom of the tin and roast for 1 hour–1 hour 20 minutes, until golden brown and the juices run clear when you push a skewer into a largest and juiciest part of the chicken leg. You can also test by using a digital thermometer until it gives an internal meat temperature of 75°C/167°F. Add a splash more liquid to the pan throughout the cooking time if the pan looks in danger of drying out.

9. Allow the chicken to rest for 20 minutes before carving and serving with the soft onions and juices from the pan.

Provençale Chicken with Rosé and Lavender

Serves 4

1 whole chicken (about 1.5kg/3lb 5oz)
juice of 1 lemon
60g (2¼oz) runny honey
60ml (2fl oz) olive oil
150ml (5fl oz) rosé wine
2 garlic cloves, crushed
1 tbsp herbes de Provence with lavender

Credit here goes to Nigella Lawson. I have many of her wonderful books, and this recipe, for St Tropez chicken, caught my eye during my one-pan chicken research. Rosé wine (ideally from Provence), honey, quite a bit of olive oil and a heady pinch of herbes de Provence - to include the crucial Provençale seasoning of dried lavender - make this a roast chicken to cook when thoughts of summer holidays start to whir. It is a messy business to marinate the whole chicken in all that wine, so a compostable plastic bag is useful in this situation. I have kept the chicken whole to roast; Nigella joints hers.

1. Put the chicken in a compostable plastic bag. Add the lemon juice, honey, oil, wine, garlic and herbs, coat well and chill overnight or for up to 2 days. Remove the chicken from the fridge about 20 minutes before you plan to cook it.

2. Preheat the oven to 180°C/160°C fan/350°F/Gas 4.

3. When you're ready to cook, place the chicken and all the marinade into a large, deep roasting tin, skin-side up. Cover the pan with some foil and roast for 1 hour-1 hour 20 minutes, until the juices run clear when you push a skewer into a largest and juiciest part of the chicken leg. You can also test by using a digital thermometer to give an internal meat temperature of 75°C/167°F.

4. Remove the foil and turn the heat up to 210°C/190°C fan/415°F/Gas 6-7 to cook for a final 10-15 minutes to brown the skin.

5. Allow the chicken to rest for 20 minutes before carving, straining any cooking juices to serve.

Goan-style Green Chicken

Serves 4

1 large bunch of coriander (cilantro), roughly chopped
2 garlic cloves, finely chopped
2–3 green chillies, to taste
1 tbsp grated (shredded) fresh ginger
2 tsp ground toasted cumin
1 tsp ground turmeric
½ tsp ground green cardamom seeds
½ tsp ground cinnamon
pinch each of ground cloves and star anise (or ground fennel)
2 tbsp poppy seeds
2 tbsp white wine or cider vinegar
1 tbsp vegetable oil
1 tsp salt, plus more to season
1 whole chicken (about 1.5kg/3lb 5oz), spatchcocked (ask your butcher to do this for you if you prefer)
1 red onion, cut into 1cm (½in) slices
freshly ground black pepper

This is my take on a Goan dish, known as Cafreal chicken. A southern Indian curry preparation, it is made with cardamom, cinnamon, ginger, chilli, coriander and vinegar, among other ingredients. Originally thought to have been introduced to the Goan state by Portuguese and African soldiers during the Portuguese conquest in 1510, it is a dish with a fascinating and cosmopolitan lineage, indicative of the tumult at the time. Still popular to this day, Goan Green Chicken is a preparation long synonymous with the region.

1. Blend half the coriander (cilantro) together with the garlic, green chillies, ginger, ground spices, poppy seeds, vinegar, oil, 1 teaspoon of salt and a generous grinding of black pepper to form a smooth sauce.

2. Mix the chicken into the sauce, cover and leave to marinate in the fridge for at least 1 hour, although the longer the better. Remove the chicken from the fridge about 20 minutes before you plan to cook it. Alternatively, forgo the marinating time and continue with the method below.

3. Preheat the oven to 200°C/180°C fan/400°F/Gas 6.

4. Place the onion in a deep roasting tray and place the chicken on top, then add 1cm (½in) water.

5. Roast the chicken for 35–45 minutes, or until cooked through, with good colour and beginning to char around the edges.

6. Remove from the oven and allow to rest for 10 minutes before serving topped with the remaining chopped coriander.

Chicken with Pistachios and Sour Cherries

Serves 4

1 red onion, cut into 1cm (½in) slices
100g (3½oz) Greek yogurt
1 tsp orange blossom water,
  or use rosewater
2 pinches of saffron, soaked in 1 tbsp
  warm water
¼ tsp ground nutmeg
½ tsp ground cinnamon
½ tsp ground green cardamom seeds
2 garlic cloves, roughly chopped
1 tsp salt, plus more to season
freshly ground black pepper
1 whole chicken (about 1.5kg/3lb 5oz),
  spatchcocked (ask your butcher to do
  this for you if you prefer)

To serve
60g (2¼oz) pistachios, ground to a
  coarse powder
50g (1¾oz) dried sour cherries,
  roughly chopped (or you could also
  use barberries)
1 tsp sumac powder
1 small bunch of mint, leaves picked and
  roughly chopped

Do try and get hold of sumac for this recipe. Sumac is the ground and dried berries from the sumac tree. With a deep, cherry-red colour, sumac has a sharp, acidic and fruity flavour. Used in lieu, or in combination with lemon or other citrus fruits, sumac is a terrific ingredient to have in your storecupboard and will suit a number of different dishes, this chicken recipe included.

1. Blend a quarter of the onion with the yogurt, orange blossom or rosewater, the saffron and its soaking liquid, the spices, the garlic, the 1 teaspoon of salt and the black pepper.

2. Mix the chicken into the sauce, cover and leave to marinate in the fridge for at least 1 hour, although the longer the better. Remove the chicken from the fridge about 20 minutes before you plan to cook it. Alternatively, forgo the marinating time and continue with the method below.

3. Preheat the oven to 200°C/180°C fan/400°F/Gas 6.

4. Place the remaining onion in a deep roasting tray and place the chicken on top, then add 1cm (½in) water.

5. Roast the chicken for 35–45 minutes, or until cooked through with good colour and beginning to char around the edges.

6. Allow to rest for 10 minutes, then serve strewn with the pistachios, cherries, sumac and mint.

FRYING
PAN

Garlic Butter Brick Chicken

Serves 4

1 whole chicken (about 1.5kg/3lb 5oz), spatchcocked (ask your butcher to do this for you if you prefer)
5 tbsp olive oil
2 tsp finely chopped rosemary leaves
2 garlic cloves, crushed
finely grated zest and juice of 1 unwaxed lemon
salt and freshly ground black pepper

You will also need
1 or 2 clean-ish bricks wrapped in a few layers of foil, depending on the size of your pan or chicken – the chicken needs to be uniformly flat

This is a brilliant method for a spatchcocked chicken. The bricks weigh down the chicken as it cooks in the pan, keeping the meat compact and extra-juicy with as much surface area as possible in contact with the heat in the pan. The result is a crisp, evenly bronzed chicken skin. My guess is you'll be using bricks in your cooking more than you ever thought possible!

1. Place the chicken on your work surface, skin-side up. Using your palms, press firmly on the breastbone to flatten the breast.

2. Rub the chicken all over with 2 tablespoons of the oil and season well with salt and pepper.

3. Mix together the rosemary, garlic and lemon zest and juice, along with 2 tablespoons of the remaining oil, in a small bowl.

4. Heat a large, ovenproof frying pan over a low-moderate heat and add the final tablespoon of oil.

5. Place the chicken, skin-side down in the frying pan, then place the bricks on top of the chicken, pressing the chicken in a level and even fashion to cook over a low-medium heat for about 10–15 minutes, until the skin browns and crisps nicely.

6. Remove the bricks from the pan and discard. Flip the chicken, brush it all over with half of the rosemary and garlic mixture and cook skin-side up for 5 minutes.

7. Meanwhile, preheat the oven to 200°C/180°C fan/400°F/ Gas 6.

8. Now cook the chicken, turning every 5 minutes or so, without the bricks weighing it down, for 20–25 minutes. Next, transfer the pan to the hot oven for 10 minutes, until the chicken is cooked through, and the juices run clear when you push a skewer into a largest and juiciest part of the chicken leg. You can also test by using a digital thermometer until it gives an internal meat temperature of 75°C/167°F.

9. Remove from the oven, drizzle all over with any of the remaining lemon and rosemary butter, then rest in a warm place for at least 10 minutes before carving and serving.

Chicken and Chorizo

Serves 4

600g (1lb 5oz) boneless, skinless chicken (thigh is best), diced
250g (9oz) cooking chorizo, casings removed and roughly chopped
2 tbsp olive oil, plus more if needed
1 red (bell) pepper, deseeded and sliced into 1cm (½in) strips
2 thick slices of day-old bread (about 100g/3½oz), crusts removed, torn into small pieces (about 1-2cm/½-¾in)
2 garlic cloves, finely sliced
1 x 400g (14oz) can of chickpeas (garbanzos), rinsed and drained
2 tsp sherry vinegar or red wine vinegar
½ small bunch of flat-leaf parsley, leaves roughly chopped
salt and freshly ground black pepper

The chorizo is first rendered in the pan, with the fat then used to cook the chicken and sliced peppers. Heavy with paprika, the chorizo fat lends a vivid colour and powerful flavour to this dish, which is based on the Spanish dish of *migas*. Many bread-eating cuisines have recipes that make use of old bread, giving a lifeline to any stale bread, soaking then toasting as the bread does here in the chorizo fat and chicken juices. A simple green salad would be a fabulous accompaniment.

1. Season the chicken with salt and pepper.

2. In a frying pan, fry the chorizo in the oil over a high heat until browned and the fat has begun to run out, remove the chorizo from the pan, leaving the fat behind, and keep to one side on a plate.

3. Add the chicken and (bell) pepper to the pan with the chorizo fat and cook over a moderate heat for around 12-15 minutes, until nicely coloured and the chicken is cooked through. Remove from the pan, keeping any fat behind once again, and keep to one side with the chorizo somewhere warm.

4. Add the bread to the pan, and just a splash more olive oil if you think it needs it, and fry the bread for around 5 minutes, until it has absorbed all the fat and has begun to toast nicely.

5. Add the garlic and cook for around 45 seconds more, then return the chorizo and chicken and peppers, along with any resting juices, to the pan.

6. Add the chickpeas (garbanzos) and cook over a moderate heat for 2 minutes - enough just to warm the chickpeas through. Remove from the heat, then add the sherry or red wine vinegar and scatter with parsley before serving.

Chicken with Fried Peaches, Bacon and Basil

Serves 4

1kg (2lb 4oz) chicken breasts
1 tbsp Dijon mustard
2 tbsp runny honey
3 tbsp red or white wine vinegar
3 tbsp olive oil
4 rashers streaky bacon, each cut
  into about 5 pieces
1 red onion, thinly sliced
3 ripe peaches, stoned and cut
  into sixths
salt and freshly ground black pepper
a big handful of basil, leaves torn,
  to serve

This is an epic chicken salad, and I use the word 'salad' with a glint in my eye. Fried peaches, bacon and chicken, this is a dish to serve just warm or at room temperature on a hot summer's day when long sunny lunches - better still long, light evenings - dictate our eating habits. Serve it with good bread to shovel and mop.

1. Season the chicken all over with salt and pepper.

2. Mix the mustard with half the honey and half the vinegar, then season with salt and pepper and put to one side.

3. In a frying pan, cook the chicken in 1 tablespoon of the olive oil skin-side down for about 5-7 minutes, until golden brown. Flip the breasts and cook them for another 3-5 minutes. Next, add the bacon and continue cooking, flipping the chicken every couple of minutes, until the chicken is fully cooked through and the bacon has crisped up. Remove both chicken and bacon from the pan to a plate, leaving the fat behind.

4. Add the onion to the pan with the fat and cook over a moderate-high heat for 5 minutes, until just softened and beginning to take on good colour. Add the remaining vinegar and cook until the vinegar is cooked away. Remove from the heat and scrape the onions onto the plate with the cooked chicken.

5. Wipe out the pan. Add the remaining olive oil and set the pan over a moderate-high heat. Add the peach slices and cook for about 1 minute on each side, then add the remaining tablespoon of honey. Fry for 45 seconds-1 minute, until nicely coloured and caramelized. Remove from the heat and put to one side.

6. Slice the chicken and arrange it on a serving plate with the bacon, onion and peaches, along with any resting juices. Drizzle the dressing over the top, then scatter with the torn basil leaves. Serve straight away.

Chicken Piccata

Serves 4

2 large boneless, skinless chicken
  breasts, sliced in half horizontally
40g (1½oz) plain (all-purpose) flour
  plus 2 tsp
70g (2½oz) butter
2 garlic cloves, finely chopped
1 shallot, finely chopped
100ml (3½fl oz) dry white wine
150ml (5fl oz) chicken stock or water
juice of ½ unwaxed lemon, plus 1 fat
  strip of the zest
25g (1oz) capers, drained if pickled;
  rinsed well and drained if salted
½ small bunch of flat-leaf parsley,
  leaves finely chopped
salt and freshly ground black pepper

Italian-American in origin, this is one of those classic dishes that remains extremely popular with home cooks and restaurants alike. I've ditched the need for breadcrumbs, opting to give the chicken a quick dredge in some seasoned flour before frying to ensure crisp, but still juicy, chicken. The best part of this recipe is the sauce, made in the pan as the chicken rests with some capers, lemon, white wine and a touch more flour to thicken. Simple and elegant, serve this with your favourite potato side dish, or some buttered pasta or noodles. Any leftovers are great stuffed in a sandwich.

1. Place each piece of chicken between two pieces of baking paper and use a heavy flat object or rolling pin to beat them out firmly but gently to an even thickness of about 5mm–1cm (¼–½in) thick.

2. Season the chicken all over with salt and pepper, then dredge it in the 40g (1½oz) of flour, shaking to remove any excess.

3. Melt the butter in a frying pan over a moderate heat. Cook the chicken for about 4 minutes each side, until nicely golden brown and crisp in places. Remove the chicken from the heat and keep it somewhere warm on a plate. Keep any fat in the pan.

4. Add the garlic and shallot to the pan and cook for about 2 minutes over a moderate heat, until softened and fragrant.

5. Stir in the 2 teaspoons of flour, mixing the flour into any fat and pan juices to form a roux. Cook this out for 1 minute, until thickened and bubbling, then add the wine, whisking well as the mixture boils and thickens for a couple of minutes over a moderate heat. Do this until the sauce has reduced by half. Don't take your eyes off the pan, and whisk often.

6. Add the chicken stock or water, and the lemon zest and juice and cook for 2 minutes, until the sauce has reduced by half again. Remove the pan from the heat and add the capers and parsley. Check the seasoning and adjust to taste.

7. Return the chicken to the pan, spooning over the sauce to warm the chicken through. Remove it from the heat and serve.

Chicken Jalfrezi

Serves 4

700g (1lb 9oz) boneless, skinless chicken
(thigh is best), diced
1 tbsp medium or hot curry powder
½–1 tsp chilli flakes or powder, to taste
2 tsp mustard seeds
1 tsp salt, plus more to season
2 onions, thinly sliced
3 garlic cloves, sliced
1 tbsp grated (shredded) fresh ginger
juice of 1 lemon
2 tbsp vegetable oil
2 tsp cumin seeds
1 cinnamon stick (about 10cm/4in)
2 (bell) peppers (any colour), deseeded
and sliced into 1cm (½in) strips
2 ripe tomatoes, each cut into 6 wedges
2 tsp garam masala
freshly ground black pepper
sliced fresh green chillies (as many
as you like), to serve

An Indian dish, specifically from the region of West Bengal, jalfrezi is said to have been devised by Indian cooks during the English-Indian occupation. It is claimed to have been a way of using up leftover roasted meats by quickly stir-frying them with onions and spices. It is a great dish (with a chequered history), and to this day many British-Indian restaurants claim it as one of their best-selling dishes. Jalfrezi translates as 'hot-fry' so keep this in mind; it is a drier style than many of the soupy, sauce-heavy curries.

1. Mix the chicken together with the curry powder, chilli flakes or powder, half the mustard seeds and ½ teaspoon of the salt.

2. Using a blender, blend half the onions, along with all the garlic and the ginger with half the lemon juice, to create a paste.

3. Heat the oil in a frying pan over a moderate-high heat. Add the cumin seeds, cinnamon stick and the remaining mustard seeds and fry for 30 seconds, until the seeds begin to pop.

4. Lower the heat to moderate, add the remaining sliced onions and fry for around 8–10 minutes, until the onions are soft.

5. Add the blended onion paste and continue to fry over a moderate heat for another 10 minutes to thicken.

6. Add the sliced (bell) peppers, the remaining ½ teaspoon of salt and the chicken. Turn up the heat to high and stir-fry for a couple of minutes.

7. Put a lid on the pan, reduce the heat back to moderate and cook for 10–12 minutes, stirring often to scrape up any sticky bits, until the chicken has cooked through and the mixture is beginning to caramelize a little in the pan.

8. Add the tomatoes, stir well, and cook for a further 2 minutes so the tomato softens but does not break down completely. You can add a tiny splash of water if the mixture begins to stick too much or catches. Check the seasoning and adjust if needed.

9. Remove from the heat and drizzle over the remaining lemon juice, then dust all over with the garam masala and strew with the chopped fresh chillies.

Chicken Fajita

Serves 4

1–3 tbsp chipotle paste or 1–3 tsp
  chipotle flakes, to taste
1 tsp smoked paprika
1 tsp ground cumin
1 tsp freshly ground black pepper
½ tsp salt
3 tbsp olive or vegetable oil
1 garlic clove, crushed
juice of 1 lime
700g (1lb 9oz) boneless, skinless chicken
  (thigh is best), diced
1 onion, finely sliced
2 red (bell) peppers, deseeded and
  sliced into 2cm (¾in) strips
2 green (bell) peppers, deseeded and
  sliced into 2cm (¾in) strips
1–2 fresh jalapeños, very thinly sliced
  (deseeded if you want less heat)

To serve
1 small bunch of coriander (cilantro),
  leaves roughly chopped
1 avocado, peeled, stoned and sliced
1 lime, cut into wedges

From the Texan boarder, this is American-influenced cooking with Mexican food in mind, used sometimes with disparaging connotations. To distinguish this style of cooking from true Mexican cooking, Tex-Mex is not without its own legacy and trademark authenticity. The use of chilli, cumin and smoked paprika, along with peppers and grated cheddar-style cheese, and served with salsas and fresh lime, creates Tex-Mex dishes of national, even worldwide, significance. Chicken suits this fajita very well – serve it with warm tortillas or rice.

1. In a large bowl, mix the spices and salt with 1 tablespoon of the oil, the garlic and the lime juice.

2. Add the chicken and mix well to combine. Set aside for at least 1 hour.

3. Heat 1 tablespoon of the remaining olive oil in a large frying pan over a moderate heat, then add the chicken and cook for 10–12 minutes, stirring often, until cooked through. Set aside on a plate, keeping the fat in the pan.

4. Add the final tablespoon of oil to the pan and stir-fry the onion over a moderate heat for around 8 minutes, until soft. Add the peppers and half the jalapeño and stir-fry for a further 5–7 minutes, until the peppers are softened, but still have a little texture.

5. Add the chicken back to the pan, mix through for a minute over a high heat and then remove the pan from the heat. Serve the chicken and peppers topped with the chopped coriander (cilantro) and sliced avocado and the remaining jalapeño, with the lime wedges for squeezing over at the table.

Chicken with Parma Ham, Sage and Grapes

Serves 4

2 large boneless, skinless chicken
   breasts, sliced in half horizontally
8 sage leaves, plus 4 more for the pan
50g (1¾oz) butter, chilled and diced,
   plus more to cook, if necessary
4 prosciutto slices
plain (all-purpose) flour, seasoned well
   with salt and pepper, for dusting
300g (10½oz) seedless black grapes
about 2 tbsp dry white wine or sherry

You will also need
4 cocktail sticks

I'm a big fan of grapes and sage as a flavour combination. Add chicken and parma ham and you're on track for a dish that is as memorable as is it delicious. Serve simply with some boiled green beans or any green vegetables and your favourite potato, or even a polenta side dish.

1. Place each chicken piece between two pieces of baking paper and use a heavy flat object or rolling pin to firmly but gently beat them until they are 5mm-1cm (¼-½in) thick.

2. Lay 2 sage leaves flat on each piece of chicken, add a small knob of the butter on top, then wrap a slice of prosciutto around each piece and secure it with a cocktail stick.

3. Dust each rolled chicken piece with the seasoned flour and brush off any excess (the flour will help with crisping and colouring the chicken nicely).

4. Melt the remaining butter in a large frying pan over a moderate heat until it is just starting to foam.

5. Add the wrapped chicken and the extra sage leaves to the pan and cook for 3-4 minutes, until the chicken is golden on one side. Turn them over to cook on the other side and spoon them all over with the foaming butter and any of the cooking juices. Cook for 3-5 minutes, until both sides are golden brown and the chicken is cooked through. Remove the chicken and sage leaves from the pan and put them to one side on a plate somewhere warm.

6. Return the pan to the heat, add the grapes and cook over a moderate heat for 2-3 minutes, until just beginning to collapse. Add the wine or sherry and reduce the liquid in the pan by half, return the chicken to the pan and spoon over the sauce. Remove from the heat and scatter with the pan-fried sage to serve.

Fried Chicken and Kimchi

Serves 4

20g (¾oz) light brown soft sugar
3 tbsp dark soy sauce
2 garlic cloves, very finely chopped
2 tbsp finely grated (shredded)
  fresh ginger
1–2 tsp chilli flakes, preferably Korean,
  to taste
2 tbsp cornflour (corn starch)
½ tsp freshly ground black pepper
700g (1lb 9oz) boneless, skinless chicken
  (thigh is best), diced
2 tbsp vegetable oil
1 red onion, finely chopped
200g (7oz) kimchi, sliced
1 tbsp toasted sesame oil
1 tbsp gochujang (Korean hot
  pepper paste)
½ bunch of spring onions (scallions),
  trimmed and thinly sliced
1 tbsp toasted sesame seeds
salt

I don't think a day passes when I don't have some kimchi in the fridge here at home. I honestly love the stuff and find it is an indispensable and favourite condiment of mine. Fridge-cold and straight from the fork is just fine as a snack for me. Frying kimchi, however, as in this recipe, will alter the flavour profile and make for a less pungent, less sour ingredient. In this case, its flavours complement the chicken beautifully, along with the ginger, sesame and soy – every ingredient working in harmony. Please don't baulk at the quantity of sugar – this is necessary for the balance of sweet and sour and all-essential caramelization.

1. Mix together the sugar, soy sauce, garlic, ginger and half the chilli flakes with 2 tablespoons of water and put to one side.

2. Season the cornflour (corn starch) with the remaining chilli flakes, a big pinch of salt and the ½ teaspoon of black pepper. Toss the chicken in the seasoned cornflour.

3. Heat the oil in a frying pan over a moderate heat and then add the chicken. Fry for 8–10 minutes, or until the chicken is just cooked through and has taken on some nice colour. Then, stir in the soy sauce mixture and bring the contents of the pan to a rapid simmer. Spoon the sauce over the chicken to coat. Remove the pan from the heat and place the chicken in a bowl to one side. Wipe out the pan.

4. Return the pan to a moderate heat and fry the onion for 2 minutes to soften and lightly brown. Then, add the kimchi, sesame oil and gochujang and cook for a further 2–3 minutes, until the onion is softened.

5. Serve the chicken with the fried onion and kimchi all strewn with the sliced spring onions (scallions) and sesame seeds.

Fried Chicken with Lettuce, Baby Onions, Bacon and Peas

Serves 4

2 tbsp olive oil
700g (1lb 9oz) boneless, skinless chicken
   (thigh is best), diced
80g (2¾oz) smoked bacon, cut into
   lardons
200g (7oz) baby or silverskin onions,
   peeled
25g (1oz) butter
2 garlic cloves, finely chopped
1 bunch of spring onions (scallions),
   trimmed and cut into 2cm (¾in) batons
2 baby gem lettuces, cut into quarters
   lengthways
150ml (5fl oz) chicken stock or water
250g (9oz) fresh or frozen peas
½ bunch of flat-leaf parsley, leaves
   picked and finely chopped
80g (2¾oz) crème fraîche
salt and freshly ground black pepper

There's a nod to the classic French dish of Petits Pois a la Française here, but yes, you guessed it, I've added chicken. Ideally, you'd have some new season peas to make this dish, but as we all know, frozen peas are often in better nick than the often too large and mealy fresh. So, I'll leave that up to you. I've also taken the liberty of adding bacon and crème fraîche, stretching even further from the origins of this recipe, but I hope you'll agree this does, absolutely, make an awful lot of sense.

1. Heat the oil in a large frying pan over a high heat and cook the chicken for 5 minutes, until it's beginning to colour nicely. Then, stir in the bacon and the onions, reduce the heat and cook until the bacon fat begins to render. Increase the heat again and cook until the bacon is nicely crisp and coloured and the onions are cooked.

2. Add the butter and garlic to the pan, reduce the heat to moderate and cook for 1 minute, until fragrant, then add the spring onions (scallions) and gem lettuces and cook for 2 minutes more, enough to just wilt.

3. Add the stock and carefully shuffle the ingredients in the pan into an even layer. Continue to cook until the chicken is cooked through, and the gems are tender but still have some shape. Turn them over halfway through cooking.

4. Add the peas and the parsley and simmer until the peas are heated through. Finally, stir through the crème fraîche and season to taste with salt and plenty of freshly ground black pepper.

Sichuan Chicken with Peanuts and Spring Onion

Serves 4

700g (1lb 9oz) boneless, skinless chicken (thigh is best), diced
2 tsp ground Sichuan pepper (optional but thoroughly recommended)
2 tbsp cornflour (corn starch)
2 tbsp light soy sauce
2 tsp Shaoxing wine or dry sherry
2 tbsp caster (superfine) sugar
2 tbsp black rice vinegar
2 tsp toasted sesame oil
4 star anise
2 tbsp toasted sesame seeds
4 tbsp sunflower or vegetable oil
8-12 small dried chillies, stem and most of the seeds discarded, then roughly chopped
1 tbsp grated (shredded) fresh ginger
4 garlic cloves, thinly sliced
1 bunch of spring onions (scallions), trimmed and cut into similar lengths as the chicken
80g (2¾oz) roasted peanuts, roughly crushed
salt

My stepmother, Lily, when I told her that my next book would be dedicated solely to chicken, insisted I include this – her recipe for Gong Bao Chicken, also known as Kung Pao Chicken. Lily is Sichuanese, and while she lives in the UK now, she has cooked me this dish to eat both here at home and, on several occasions, in Chengdu, alongside her brothers and sisters. When Lily makes this, which is often, it is so very delicious - it is almost as if the chicken leaves the fridge and is there cooked on the table, indescribably glossy, in 10 minutes flat, with us all waiting giddy, rice at the ready, with greedy pleasure.

1. Season the chicken with a big pinch of salt and the Sichuan pepper, then dust with half the cornflour (corn starch), to coat. Next, add 1 tablespoon of the soy sauce and all the Shaoxing wine or sherry and mix well.

2. In a bowl, mix together the sugar, vinegar and sesame oil, along with 2 tablespoons of water, the star anise, sesame seeds and the remaining soy sauce and cornflour. Put to one side.

3. Heat the oil in a wok or large frying pan over a high heat. Add the dried chillies and stir-fry for about 20 seconds, then add the chicken and stir-fry for a few minutes. Add the ginger, garlic and spring onions (scallions) and cook for 5-7 minutes, until the chicken is just cooked through.

4. Mix through the vinegar mixture, stir-frying over a high heat for a couple of minutes to fully coat and cook the chicken.

5. Remove from the heat and scatter with the crushed peanuts to serve.

STOCKPOT

Chicken and Rice Soup

Serves 4

3 tbsp olive oil, plus more to serve
1 onion, finely diced
1 green (bell) pepper, finely diced
4 garlic cloves: 3 thinly sliced, 1 very
    finely chopped
500g (1lb 2oz) boneless, skinless chicken
    (thigh is best), diced
½ tsp salt, plus more to season
200g (7oz) tomato, grated, or use
    chopped canned
1 tbsp tomato purée (paste)
good pinch of saffron, soaked in 2 tbsp
    warm water
100g (3½oz) paella rice, or another
    short grain rice
1.5 litres (52fl oz) chicken stock
2 tbsp ground almonds
½ small bunch of flat-leaf parsley,
    leaves finely chopped
freshly ground black pepper

I love using short grain rice in soups and broths. I like how the rice swells as it cooks in the liquid, but still maintains a pleasing chewy, toothsome texture. If you don't have paella rice, you could equally use short grain pudding rice or risotto rice. I've stated paella rice here because I am looking broadly to Spain – to Catalan cooking in particular – where a mixture of pounded nuts, parsley and garlic (called a picada) is often used to thicken soups, stews and braises. I've simplified this by using ground almonds; by all means pound whole almonds with the parsley and garlic to add to the finished soup, if you prefer.

1. Heat the olive oil in a large pot over a moderate heat. Add the onion and (bell) pepper and cook for around 8 minutes, until softened, then add the sliced garlic and the chicken with the ½ teaspoon of salt and cook for 10 minutes, stirring often and turning the chicken over, until the chicken is beginning to colour all over and the vegetables are soft and just slightly sticking to the base of the pan (scrape often).

2. Add the tomato, tomato purée (paste) and the saffron with its soaking liquid and cook for 5 minutes, until rich and thick.

3. Add the rice and chicken stock, then bring the liquid to a boil. Turn down the heat to moderate and simmer for about 20 minutes, until the rice is tender (give the contents of the pan a good stir every now and then, so the rice doesn't catch or clump together – you want it to thicken the stock just slightly as it cooks).

4. Stir through the almonds, parsley and chopped garlic, then check the seasoning, adding more salt and pepper, if necessary.

5. Remove from the heat and serve each bowl drizzled with a little extra olive oil.

Chicken Ramen

Serves 4

For the base

3 pieces of dried kombu (dried kelp; optional but recommended)

8 dried shiitake mushrooms

1.5 litres (52fl oz) chicken stock

500g (1lb 2oz) boneless, skinless chicken (thigh is best), diced

300g (10½oz) ramen noodles

1 tbsp sake (optional, but worth it)

1 tbsp mirin

2 tbsp light soy sauce

2–3 tbsp white miso

any green vegetables – such as baby spinach, pak choi or kale, thinly sliced

Toppings

4 spring onions (scallions), thinly sliced

2 tsp Japanese seven spice (togarashi; optional, but again, worth it), or use ½–1 tsp dried chilli flakes, to taste

Ramen is a Japanese preparation, an authentic version of which might take you several days to create. A *tonkotsu* broth, for example, will require hours of slowly braising trotters and more to extract the creamy, sticky collagen. Meticulous attention to detail is required for a properly made ramen. There are then, also those packets found in supermarkets and all Asian grocery stores. Immense in variety, these individually portioned waffly slabs of semi-cooked then dried noodles come complete with a small metallic sachet to sprinkle. These packets will have you believe ramen, or rather, an approximation of ramen, is ready in 4 minutes flat. This recipe falls somewhere between the two! I've suggested you source some kombu for the ramen broth - it is an essential ramen ingredient and available in all Asian grocery stores and also online.

1. Soak the kombu and mushrooms in 400ml (14fl oz) of cold water for at least 1 hour or up to 2 days in advance in the fridge.

2. After soaking, place the shiitake and kombu with their soaking water in a large pot with the chicken stock and heat slowly until just coming to a boil. Remove the kombu and discard. Remove the shiitake, thinly slice it and put it to one side.

3. Bring the liquid to a simmer, then add the chicken and gently simmer over a moderate heat for 15–20 minutes, until the chicken is just cooked through. Then, add the noodles, sake, mirin, soy sauce and miso and simmer for just 2–3 minutes more, until the noodles are tender.

4. Add the green vegetables and return the sliced shiitake to the broth to heat through.

5. Divide the cooked noodles between your bowls and ladle over the hot ramen broth, distributing the noodles, chicken, shiitake and green vegetables evenly, before topping with the sliced spring onions (scallions) and togarashi (or chilli flakes), if using, which I recommend you do. Serve piping hot.

Chicken Soup with Lime Leaf, Lemongrass and Coconut

Serves 4

1.5 litres (52fl oz) chicken stock
4 lime leaves, thinly sliced
3 lemongrass stalks, trimmed and cut
   into thirds
3-6 bird's-eye red or green chillies,
   ½ thinly sliced, ½ left whole, to taste
4 slices fresh galangal (or ginger)
½ small bunch coriander (cilantro),
   leaves (chopped) and stalks separated
150g (5½oz) cherry tomatoes, cut in half
200ml (7fl oz) full-fat coconut milk
400g (14oz) boneless, skinless chicken
   (thigh is best), diced
150g (5½oz) small button mushrooms
juice of 2 limes
2 tbsp fish sauce, plus more to taste

This soup is based on a Thai coconut soup known as Tom Kah Gai or Tom Kah Kai, a sour, fragrant soup made with chicken, coconut milk, lime leaves, lemongrass and fresh chilli. It is simply delicious - all at once vibrant and refreshing, soothing and restorative. I have eaten similar soups to this on various trips to Thailand, but also in Cambodia and Laos. Each time, with each bowlful, I swear it is the best chicken soup I'll eat.

1. Heat the chicken stock in a large pot over a high heat.

2. Meanwhile bruise the lime leaves, lemongrass, whole chillies, galangal (or ginger) and coriander (cilantro) stalks in a mortar and pestle (or use a bowl and the end of a rolling pin), then add them along with the tomatoes to the hot stock and simmer for 5 minutes.

3. Add the coconut milk, chicken and mushrooms, bring the liquid back to a boil, then reduce the heat to moderate and cook for about 5-8 minutes, until the chicken is cooked through.

4. Remove from the heat and add the sliced chillies, lime juice, fish sauce and chopped coriander leaves, adjusting with more of each, to your taste. Serve ladled into bowls immediately.

Hot Sour Soup

Serves 4

300g (10½oz) boneless, skinless chicken (thigh is best), diced
2 tbsp dark soy sauce
1 tsp caster (superfine) or light brown soft sugar
2 tbsp cornflour (corn starch)
2 tbsp vegetable oil
1 tbsp grated (shredded) fresh ginger
1 carrot, coarsely grated, or cut into very thin matchsticks
4 bamboo shoots (canned is fine), drained and thinly sliced
4 dried shiitake mushrooms, soaked in hot water for 30 minutes, then drained and thinly sliced
1 small handful of dried wood ear mushrooms, soaked in hot water for at least 30 minutes, then drained and thinly sliced
1.5 litres (52fl oz) chicken stock
200g (3½oz) soft tofu, cut into 2cm cubes
3 tbsp black rice vinegar, such as Chinkiang
salt and freshly ground white pepper (or use black pepper)

To serve
2 spring onions (scallions), trimmed and finely sliced
2 tsp sesame oil

When I was working out in Chengdu in China a few years ago and living with my stepmother, Lily, it was Lily's passion for soup making and eating that really got me into using an assortment of dried mushrooms in so many different broths, soups and braises that I cook here at home. The wood ear mushroom is a case in point. Dried, this ingredient looks rather unremarkable. But, rehydrated, the wood ear plumps to a wonderful dark, lustrous ruffle of a fungus, with a chewy, almost slippery texture. Flavour-wise, wood ear is mild and earthy tasting. These mushrooms are a must if you want to add (and you absolutely must) some all-important texture to a soup such as this one. Wood ear, sometimes sold as black fungus, can often be found in larger Asian supermarkets and online. Lily now lives in the UK and was thrilled to spot some wood ear growing on a damp, mossy log while on a foraging walk with a friend one day in Cornwall.

1. Mix the chicken with half each of the soy sauce, sugar and cornflour (corn starch).

2. Heat the oil in a pot over a moderate heat, then add the chicken and fry for 5–7 minutes, until just cooked through.

3. Add the ginger, carrot, bamboo shoots, and all the soaked and sliced mushrooms and cook for 1 minute over a high heat, then add the chicken stock, bring the liquid to a boil and simmer for 5 minutes.

4. Mix the remaining cornflour with the remaining soy sauce and sugar and stir this slurry into the soup, along with plenty of freshly ground white pepper to taste. Cook, while stirring, for 2 minutes for the cornflour to thicken the soup. Add the tofu to the pot and warm through.

5. Remove the pot from the heat and add the black rice vinegar. Top with the spring onions (scallions) and drizzle with some sesame oil. Taste for salt and serve immediately.

Stracciatella or Egg Drop Soup

Serves 4

3 garlic cloves, peeled
2 tbsp olive oil
1 litre (35fl oz) chicken stock
1 strip of unwaxed lemon zest
300g (10½oz) boneless, skinless chicken
   (thigh is best), diced
2 eggs, beaten
big pinch of freshly ground nutmeg
3 tbsp semolina flour (or use the same
   amount of stale fine breadcrumbs)
½ small bunch of flat-leaf parsley,
   very finely chopped
80g (2¾oz) parmesan or pecorino,
   finely grated, plus extra to serve
salt and freshly ground black pepper

Few ingredients here, and yet this soup really delivers masses in terms of simple, nurturing flavour. The egg and the nutmeg lend a sweet, creamy depth to the chicken stock, which is thickened just slightly with some semolina, then showered with freshly grated parmesan and finely chopped parsley to serve. The soup is best served when you (or the world) needs a sticking plaster – this is deeply soothing.

1. Put the garlic and the olive oil in a pot over a moderate–low heat and cook gently for 2–3 minutes, until the garlic is fragrant and beginning to ever-so lightly colour.

2. Add the stock and lemon zest. Bring the liquid to a boil, then simmer over a moderate heat for 30 minutes – long enough for the flavours to infuse.

3. Add the chicken and continue to gently simmer over a moderate heat for around 10 minutes, until the chicken is cooked through.

4. In a small bowl, season the eggs with some salt, pepper and the nutmeg. Add the semolina (or breadcrumbs), mixing well.

5. Add the egg mixture to the pan and stir well for a couple of minutes over a moderate heat – enough for the egg to ribbon in the hot stock and for the semolina to thicken it.

6. Remove the pot from the heat. Add the parsley and the grated cheese, mixing well. Grate more cheese directly into the bowls as you serve.

Poached Chicken with Freekeh

Serves 4

200g (7oz) freekeh (or use coarse bulgur
  and halve the cooking time)
1 whole chicken (about 1.5kg/3lb 5oz)
1 tsp salt, plus more to season
1 cinnamon stick (about 10cm/4in)
4 cardamom pods
8 allspice berries
10 whole black peppercorns
1 onion, halved
2 garlic cloves, peeled
½ bunch of flat-leaf parsley, leaves and
  stalks separated
4 small carrots, halved
freshly ground black pepper

To serve
½ garlic clove, crushed
150g (5½oz) Greek yogurt
flaky salt
sumac

Freekeh is durum wheat that has been processed by burning the wheat head to expose the grain within. It has a nutty, slightly smoky flavour and can be used in recipes where rice or bulgur are suggested. In this recipe, the chicken is poached with whole garlic and carrots along with the aromatics of cinnamon, cardamom and allspice to make a beautifully fragrant broth. With the cooked chicken resting and bathed in half a measure of the broth, the remaining broth is then used to cook the freekeh. Serve with seasoned yogurt and sumac.

1. Place the freekeh in a sieve and rinse it under plenty of cold water, then leave to drain.

2. With a sharp knife, slit the skin between the chicken legs and breasts – this will allow the hot liquid to circulate more freely during the cooking time.

3. Place the chicken in a pan with the teaspoon of salt, the whole spices, and the onion, garlic, parsley stalks and carrots. Cover with cold water and bring to a boil, then gently simmer for about 45 minutes–1 hour, until the chicken is cooked through. (You can also test by using a digital thermometer until it gives an internal meat temperature of 75°C/167°F.)

4. Once the chicken is cooked, remove all of the ingredients from the pan and place these in a large serving bowl to rest and keep warm, leaving just half the measure of stock back in the pot. You can discard the parsley stalks.

5. Add the rinsed freekeh to the pot with the stock, bring the liquid to a boil, then reduce the heat and simmer the freekeh for 15–20 minutes, until tender, then drain (discard the stock).

6. Mix the crushed garlic into the yogurt and season with salt and pepper.

7. Remove the chicken from the bowl and joint, then serve on top of the freekeh and carrots, strewn with chopped parsley leaves and with the seasoned yogurt, flaky sea salt and sumac on the side. You can bring the remaining half of the stock back to the boil and ladle it over the chicken and freekeh, if you wish.

Poached Whole Chicken with Leeks and Tarragon Mayo

Serves 4

1 whole chicken (about 1.5kg/3lb 5oz)
2 carrots, peeled and halved
1 onion, halved
2 garlic cloves, skin on and bashed with
  the side of a heavy knife
2 celery stalks
3 good-size and bushy tarragon stalks,
  stalks and leaves separated (see below)
1 tsp whole black peppercorns
1 tsp sea salt, plus more to taste
4 leeks, cut into 10cm (4in) lengths

For the mayonnaise
2 large egg yolks
100ml (3½fl oz) olive oil
300ml (10½fl oz) sunflower oil
splash of white wine or cider vinegar
tarragon leaves (see above),
  finely chopped
salt and freshly ground black pepper

Note:
You can cool and freeze any excess broth
and use it in any recipe that calls for
chicken stock.

Tarragon is a classic match for chicken; its faintly aniseed notes provide invigorating flavours that flatter a good and tasty bird. Here, the tarragon stalks are used in the poaching liquor and the leaves are finely chopped for the mayonnaise, which is an unbeatable accompaniment. This is a dish with elegant, old-fashioned charm. Some simply boiled potatoes would be the perfect match.

1. With a sharp knife, slit the skin between the chicken legs and breasts - this will allow the hot liquid to circulate more freely during the cooking time.

2. Place the chicken and all the ingredients apart from the leeks in a large pot and just cover with cold water. Bring to a boil, then turn down the heat to moderate-low and simmer gently for about 45 minutes–1 hour, adding the leeks about 20 minutes into the cooking time, until the chicken is cooked through to the bone. (You can also test by using a digital thermometer until it gives an internal meat temperature of 75°C/167°F.)

3. Meanwhile, make the mayonnaise. Whisk the egg yolks, a big pinch of salt and a little pepper in a bowl (or use a small food processor or blender). Put the oils in a jug (pitcher) that is easy to pour from. Then, slowly start whisking a few drops of oil into the egg mixture. Increase the quantity of oil you're adding each time, whisking in each addition so it is properly amalgamated before adding the next. Once the mayo is emulsified and holds its shape, add the oil in a thin stream, all the while whisking. Taste and check the seasoning, then add the vinegar, and season with salt and a generous amount of freshly ground black pepper. Add the chopped tarragon. Put to one side.

4. Remove the chicken and leeks from the pot, cover loosely with foil and place somewhere warm to rest.

5. Strain the stock into a jug, return it to the pot and simmer for 20 minutes to reduce by about a third. Check the seasoning and adjust as required. Remove from the heat.

6. Carve the chicken and slice the leeks. Serve each portion in shallow bowls, ladle over some of the hot chicken broth and dollop with the tarragon mayonnaise.

Chicken Soup with Egg and Lemon

Serves 4

1.6 litres (54fl oz) chicken stock
1 onion, quartered
1 leek, white and light green parts only, thickly sliced
1 celery stalk, thickly sliced
1 good-size thyme sprig
½ small bunch of dill, ½ finely chopped
400g (14oz) boneless, skinless chicken (thigh is best), diced
60g (2¼oz) white rice (short or long grain, up to you)
2 large eggs
juice of 2 lemons (about 80ml/2½fl oz)
salt and freshly ground black pepper

To Greece for inspiration with this soup, a wonderfully velvety number with the chicken stock thickened, all silky smooth, with a mixture of beaten egg and quite a bit of lemon juice. Dill and plenty of cracked black pepper for serving make for a chicken soup that is astonishing in its simplicity. It's one to eat when you need to rest and restore.

1. Put the chicken stock in a large pot with the onion, leek, celery and whole sprigs of herbs. Bring to a boil, then simmer for 5 minutes. Then, add the chicken and simmer for around 15 minutes, or until the chicken is cooked through. Transfer the cooked chicken to a bowl and leave it to cool.

2. Strain the chicken stock into a jug (pitcher) and return it to the pot. Add the rice and bring the liquid to a boil, then reduce the heat and simmer for 20 minutes, until the rice is cooked.

3. In a bowl, whisk together the eggs and the lemon juice. Slowly whisk a ladle of the hot broth into the egg mixture, whisking well, to just warm the egg and lemon mixture.

4. Then, whisking continuously, gradually add the warmed egg and lemon mixture into the stockpot and simmer gently over a moderate heat, stirring all the time until the soup has been slightly thickened by the eggs. Check the seasoning, adding salt if you think it's necessary.

5. Add the cooked chicken back to the soup and strew with the chopped dill and plenty of freshly ground black pepper to serve.

Get-Better-Soon Chicken Soup

Serves 4

600g (1lb 5oz) chicken legs or
   chicken thighs
2 bay leaves
4 carrots, peeled
4 celery stalks
1 large onion, peeled
2 litres (70fl oz) chicken stock
½ tsp salt, plus more to season
3 flat-leaf parsley sprigs, leaves
   (finely chopped) and stalks separated
200g (7oz) dried rice vermicelli or angel
   hair pasta
freshly ground black pepper

The calling card of so many of the chicken soups in this chapter is one of calming repair, to eat when gentle sustenance is needed, when nothing too troubling or with too much exertion is necessary. My mum would make chicken soup for me when I was under the weather as a child. Curled on the sofa, daytime television on, a bowl of this was a tonic, and it always will be. My mum would serve her Get-Better-Soon Chicken Soup with thick slices of bread, thickly buttered, but I've added vermicelli noodles to the rich chicken broth because, full circle, my own children now relish noodles over bread and butter, and slurping long strands from bowl to face seems to have good restorative powers of its own (or, at the very least, it can conjure a weak, tired smile).

1. Place all the ingredients, except the parsley leaves and vermicelli or pasta, in a large pot. Cover the pot with a lid and bring the liquid to a boil over a high heat.

2. Reduce the heat to low–moderate and simmer for 30–40 minutes, until the chicken is cooked through.

3. Remove the chicken and vegetables from the pot and strain the stock into a jug (pitcher). Then, return the stock to the pot and bring it back to a boil. Add the noodles and simmer them according to the packet instructions, until tender and cooked through.

4. Meanwhile pull the chicken from the bones, remove and discard the bones and the skin, then chop or shred the meat along with the carrots and celery. Add these back to the hot stock, then add the chopped parsley leaves and check the seasoning, adding more salt and freshly ground black pepper as necessary.

5. Serve immediately, ladling chicken, vegetables, noodles and plenty of broth into each bowl.

Chicken Laksa

Serves 4

2 shallots, roughly chopped
2 garlic cloves, roughly chopped
1 tbsp grated (shredded) fresh ginger
1 tbsp grated (shredded) fresh galangal,
  or use galangal paste
1 tsp shrimp paste (or 1 tbsp fish sauce),
  plus more to taste
1 tbsp light brown soft or palm sugar
2 lemongrass stalks, trimmed and
  finely chopped
40g (1½oz) cashew nuts or unsalted
  peanuts
1-2 red or green bird's-eye chillies
  (deseeded if you want less heat), to taste
2 tsp ground cumin
2 tsp ground coriander
3 tbsp coconut or sunflower oil
40g (1½oz) tamarind paste
800ml (28fl oz) chicken stock or water
1 star anise
400g (14oz) boneless, skinless chicken
  (thigh is best), diced
200ml (7fl oz) full-fat coconut milk
2 limes
150g (5½oz) dried rice vermicelli, cooked
  according to the packet instructions, or
  300g (10½oz) fresh noodles
salt

To serve
300g (10½oz) beansprouts
½ bunch of spring onions (scallions),
  finely sliced
½ cucumber, cut into thin matchsticks
1 small bunch of coriander (cilantro),
  leaves roughly chopped
chilli sauce or sambal, to taste

This is, hands down, one of the best chicken soups on earth. I'm looking to Singapore for this laksa. I have eaten laksas in Singapore, and in a Sydney pub, made by a Singaporean woman, cooked in a tiny kitchen and served out of a hatch to the pub's punters (which I should mention was the best laksa of my life), and many more at home in the UK. I honestly think being able to cook a good laksa should be on the national curriculum. For thrilling food that delivers comfort and nutrition, laksa is the ultimate dish. There are regional varieties of laksa in both Singapore and neighbouring Malaysia, with each country and its cooks all having their own take on this popular dish. This is mine.

1. Blend the shallots with the garlic, ginger, galangal, shrimp paste (or fish sauce), sugar, lemongrass, cashews or peanuts, ½ the fresh chilli and the ground spices to a smooth paste (adding a splash of water, if necessary).

2. Heat the oil in a pot and add the paste, frying for 5-10 minutes, until the paste is starting to concentrate and just beginning to stick to the bottom of the pan.

3. Stir the tamarind and the stock into the paste, add the star anise and mix together well, then bring the liquid to a boil. Add the chicken, reduce the heat and simmer for 15-20 minutes until the chicken is cooked through.

4. Stir the coconut milk into the laksa and cook for 5 minutes, then add the juice of one of the limes. Season with salt to taste.

5. Divide the cooked noodles into serving bowls.

6. Ladle the laksa over the noodles and top with the beansprouts, spring onions (scallions), cucumber, coriander (cilantro) and remaining fresh chilli. Serve with chilli sauce or sambal and the remaining lime cut into wedges on the side.

Malaysian-Style Chicken Cooked with Rice

Serves 4

1 whole chicken (about 1.5kg/3lb 5oz)
1.2 litres (40fl oz) chicken stock
2 x 1cm (½in) slices of fresh ginger, plus 2 tsp finely grated (shredded) fresh ginger
1 star anise
2 garlic cloves: 1 peeled and left whole, 1 peeled and crushed
1 lemongrass stalk, bruised with the back of a knife or rolling pin
1 bunch of spring onions (scallions), green and white parts separated, green parts thinly sliced
½ tsp salt
2 pak choi, sliced lengthways into quarters
300g (10½oz) basmati rice
1 juicy lime, halved
1 tsp dark soy sauce, plus more to serve
chilli sauce, to serve

In my twenties I travelled to Malaysia with my best friend Isabel, also a chef. It was our first trip abroad as adults, and also as chefs. We ate breakfast, lunch and dinner, adding in snacks and a vast array of street food at all possible moments. We were incredibly well fed in Malaysia. We ate many versions of chicken cooked with rice, and since that trip, this is a method I now often use to cook chicken and rice for my family.

1. With a sharp knife, slit the skin between the chicken legs and breasts – this will allow the hot liquid to circulate more freely.

2. Put the chicken stock, sliced ginger, star anise, whole garlic, lemongrass, the white parts of the spring onions (scallions) and the salt into a large pot and bring to a boil.

3. Add the chicken to the stock, then simmer for 45 minutes–1 hour, or until the chicken is cooked through. (You can also test by using a digital thermometer until it gives an internal meat temperature of 75°C/167°F.) Transfer the chicken to a large bowl, then strain the cooking liquid through a sieve into the bowl with the chicken. Cover the bowl, then discard the ingredients remaining in the sieve.

4. Measure out 600ml (21fl oz) of the stock and return it to the pot. Add the pak choi and cook over a high heat for 2 minutes, to wilt. Remove the pak choi from the liquid using a slotted spoon or tongs and place it in the bowl with the chicken.

5. Add the rice to the pan, bring to a boil, then reduce the heat to moderate. Cover the pan and cook for 12–15 minutes, or until all the stock has been absorbed and the rice is tender.

6. Meanwhile, mix the grated ginger with the juice of ½ the lime, the crushed garlic, soy sauce and 2 tablespoons of the reserved chicken stock to make a sauce. Put this to one side.

7. Joint the chicken and place a few pieces and some pak choi in each bowl. Ladle over some reserved hot stock and strew with the spring onion greens. Serve alongside the cooked rice, the ginger and lime sauce, with extra chilli sauce and soy sauce on the side. Cut the remaining lime half into wedges, for squeezing.

LEFTOVERS

Coronation Chicken Sandwich

Makes 4

2 tbsp sunflower oil

2 tsp finely grated (shredded) fresh ginger

2 tsp curry powder (mild or hot)

good pinch of ground cinnamon

good pinch of chilli powder (mild or hot), or more to taste

2 tbsp good mango chutney

juice of 1 lemon

500g (1lb 2oz) leftover cooked chicken meat, shredded or sliced

80g (2¾oz) Greek yogurt

80g (2¾oz) mayonnaise

1 ripe mango, peeled, stoned and finely diced

1 small bunch of coriander (cilantro), leaves roughly chopped

8 slices of your favourite bread

40g (1½oz) toasted flaked almonds

salt and freshly ground black pepper

Originally devised in 1953 to commemorate the coronation of Queen Elizabeth II, it's safe to say – 70+ years on and many recipes duplicated since, and not to mention its place as a stalwart filling for many a sandwich shop – coronation chicken remains an extremely popular combination. Whatever your stance on royalty and viewing the original recipe and the spices used through the prism of Anglo-Indian occupation, the combination of chicken served in a creamy, fruity, spicy dressing is an alluring, albeit enormously British, one. I've lightened the mayonnaise with Greek yogurt and added in some finely diced ripe mango for extra-fruity sass. White sliced bread, sandwiched shut, would be my preference here, although you could also serve it as a salad on top of some soft buttery lettuce leaves.

1. Heat the oil in a small pan over a low heat with the ginger and ground spices for 2 minutes, until aromatic, then stir in 1 tablespoon of the mango chutney and half the lemon juice. Remove from the heat and mix in the chicken. Ideally, allow the chicken to marinate for about 30 minutes – it's up to you.

2. Mix together the yogurt, mayonnaise and remaining tablespoon of mango chutney.

3. Combine the marinated chicken, diced mango, and half the coriander (cilantro). Season with a good pinch of salt and plenty of freshly ground black pepper, along with the remaining lemon juice.

4. Assemble the sandwich. Slather one side of the bread with the mayonnaise mixture, pile the other with the chicken mixture, top with the remaining chopped coriander and scatter over the almonds. Sandwich the bread shut and eat.

Fried Chicken and Cheese Sandwich with Kimchi and Avocado

Serves 4

50g (1¾oz) butter, softened
8 slices of good white bread
200g (7oz) cheddar cheese, grated
1 egg yolk
1 tbsp dark soy sauce
1 tbsp Dijon mustard
200g (7oz) kimchi, thinly sliced if needed
400g (14oz) leftover cooked chicken meat, shredded or sliced
2 avocados, peeled, stoned and thinly sliced
splash of olive or neutral-tasting oil, for frying
salt and freshly ground black pepper

When I assembled and fried this sandwich during the photoshoot for this cookbook, it was gone in seconds, not a scrap of it left on the chopping board. This speaks volumes, given that there is an awful lot of food to sample on a cookbook shoot. Quick to make, this is an eye-popping send-off for any leftover chicken you might have lurking in your fridge.

1. Butter one side of each slice of bread.

2. Mix together the cheese, egg yolk, soy sauce and mustard and season with black pepper, then stir in the kimchi. Season with salt (and more pepper, if you like) to taste, then add the chicken and mix well to coat.

3. Spread the chicken and kimchi mixture over the unbuttered side of 4 of the bread slices. Top with equal amounts of the avocado and sandwich shut with the buttered sides of the bread facing outwards.

4. Heat a frying pan over a medium heat with a splash of oil. Add as many sandwiches as will fit to the pan and fry, turning carefully – about 3 minutes on each side should do – until crisp and golden brown. Repeat with the remaining sandwiches, adding more oil to the pan, if necessary.

5. Drain the sandwiches on kitchen paper, cut them into pieces and serve immediately.

Caesar Salad

Serves 4

4 thick slices of sourdough or any rustic bread, torn into pieces
150ml (5fl oz) vegetable or light olive oil, plus 3 tbsp to cook the croûtons
2 garlic cloves: 1 finely crushed, 1 left whole, unpeeled and slightly bashed
6 salted anchovy fillets, drained and finely chopped
1 tsp Dijon mustard
1 tbsp white wine, red wine or cider vinegar
2 large egg yolks
40g parmesan, finely grated, plus plenty more shavings to serve
cold chicken stock or water
400g (14oz) leftover cooked chicken meat, shredded or sliced
1 large cos or romaine lettuce, or 2 little gem hearts, leaves separated and broken in half if big
salt and freshly ground black pepper

Give me salted anchovies, crisp salad leaves and croûtons with my leftover chicken. Add homemade mayonnaise made with plenty of Dijon mustard and shower the lot with parmesan shavings. If there was a hill... let a good, well-made Caesar salad lead me there!

1. Preheat the oven to 180°C/160°C fan/350°F/Gas 4. Toss the bread with the 3 tablespoons of oil and the bashed whole garlic. Place the bread pieces on a baking tray and season with salt and pepper. Bake for about 10 minutes, shuffling the bread and garlic clove midway through the cooking time, until golden and crisp. Remove from the oven and set to one side.

2. Meanwhile, whisk together the anchovies, crushed garlic, mustard, vinegar and egg yolks.

3. Start adding the 150ml (5fl oz) of oil – drop by drop to begin with, then in a very thin stream, whisking all the time until the mayonnaise is nicely thickened, rich and glossy. You can do this by hand in a bowl with a whisk or use a small food processor – just be sure to add the oil very slowly to begin with so the mayonnaise doesn't split. If it does, wipe out the bowl, and begin again with an extra egg yolk, very slowly whisking in the mix to amalgamate.

4. Add the finely grated parmesan and loosen the texture of the dressing with the cold chicken stock or water until it reaches the consistency of double (heavy) cream. Season with salt and pepper.

5. Season the leftover chicken with salt and pepper.

6. In a serving bowl mix together the lettuce, chicken and the croûtons with the dressing, lightly coating all the ingredients in the bowl. Add parmesan shavings to serve.

Chicken with Radicchio, Clementines and Walnuts

Serves 4

400g (14oz) leftover cooked chicken meat, shredded or sliced
2 tbsp red wine vinegar
½ small red onion, finely diced
1 tbsp Dijon mustard
4–5 tbsp olive oil
1 radicchio, cored and sliced into ribbons
4 clementines, peeled and thinly sliced
1 small bunch of watercress
1 small bunch of flat-leaf parsley, leaves picked and roughly chopped if large, kept whole if on the small side
50g (1¾oz) walnuts, toasted and roughly chopped
salt and freshly ground black pepper

Citrus in a salad is one of my favourite things. Bright and juicy, clementines provide an excellent canvas for this chicken salad, along with the walnuts and radicchio. Throw this all together with breathtaking insouciance, but really you and I both know, precise construction has gone on to produce a dish so beautiful your guests will stop and draw breath, every mouthful a perfect mixture.

1. Season the chicken to taste with salt and plenty of freshly ground black pepper.

2. Mix the vinegar and onion together in a small bowl and season well with salt and pepper. Add the mustard and whisk in the oil to make a dressing. Put to one side.

3. Arrange the radicchio, clementines, watercress and parsley leaves on a wide serving dish. Add the chicken and the walnuts and drizzle the dressing over the top, tossing lightly to coat. Serve immediately.

Chicken with Bashed Cucumber, Sichuan and Peanuts

Serves 4

60ml (2fl oz) vegetable or sunflower oil
5mm (¼in) slice of fresh ginger, plus
   1 tsp finely grated (shredded)
1-3 tsp chilli flakes, to taste
1½ tsp ground Sichuan peppercorns
   (or use whole, roughly crushed)
2 tbsp sesame oil
2 tbsp sesame seeds, plus more to serve
1 cucumber
1 garlic clove, finely crushed
2 tbsp black rice Chinese vinegar
   (or use white or red wine vinegar)
3 tbsp dark soy sauce
2 tsp caster (superfine) sugar or
   runny honey
2 tbsp Chinese sesame paste
   (or use tahini paste)
400g (14oz) leftover cooked chicken
   meat, shredded or sliced
½ bunch of spring onions (scallions),
   trimmed and finely sliced
50g (1¾oz) roasted peanuts,
   roughly chopped
salt

My Sichuanese stepmother Lily makes this dish often for the children and me. Over the years, the amount of chilli oil she adds has increased, with my eldest now happy to eat this dish as hot as Lily likes to eat it herself. Sichuan peppercorns have a numbing, buzzy feel in the mouth. Any fiery heat will come from how many chilli flakes you choose to add. Sichuan peppercorns, black Chinese vinegar and Chinese sesame paste are all available to buy in Chinese supermarkets and online. Tahini paste would suffice in place of the sesame paste, though, especially a darker version – but to my mind, the Sichuan peppercorns and black Chinese vinegar are non-negotiable. I am sure Lily would agree.

1. Make a chilli oil. Heat the vegetable oil with the ginger in a frying pan over a high heat. When the ginger starts to bubble, add the chilli flakes and Sichuan pepper and remove the pan from the heat. Add the sesame oil and sesame seeds, then put to one side.

2. Meanwhile, whack the cucumber firmly down its length on a chopping board with a rolling pin, until slightly bashed and split – bashed, not mashed! Slice down the length of the cucumber then slice into 2-3cm (¾-1¼in) pieces. Place the cucumber pieces in a sieve set over a bowl. Add a big pinch of salt and half the crushed garlic. Leave the cucumber like this for 15 minutes for the salt to extract the excess liquid and the garlic to marinate.

3. Meanwhile, mix 1 tablespoon of the vinegar with 1 tablespoon of the soy sauce and 1 teaspoon of the sugar or honey until dissolved. Spread the cucumber over a serving plate and pour this dressing over the cucumber, mixing lightly to coat.

4. Mix the sesame paste with the remaining 2 tablespoons of soy sauce, remaining tablespoon of vinegar, remaining teaspoon of sugar or honey, the grated ginger and the remaining garlic. Add 2 tablespoons of cold water, and mix to form a smooth, creamy dressing. Add the chicken to this dressing, then add half the chilli oil, mixing well to combine.

5. Top the cucumber with the dressed chicken then scatter with the spring onions (scallions), peanuts and extra sesame seeds. Serve the extra chilli oil on the side.

Chicken with Chipotle Mayo and Slaw

Serves 4

40g (1½oz) pumpkin seeds
80g (2¾oz) mayonnaise
80g (2¾oz) sour cream
1 small garlic clove, finely crushed
  with a little salt
1–3 tbsp chipotle paste, to taste
2 limes: 1 juiced, 1 quartered to serve
400g (14oz) leftover cooked chicken
  meat, shredded or sliced
2 carrots, peeled and grated
¼ red or white cabbage, very
  thinly sliced
4 spring onions (scallions), trimmed
  and finely sliced
1 small bunch of coriander (cilantro),
  leaves roughly chopped
4 tortilla wraps or flat breads
hot sauce, of choice, to taste
salt and freshly ground black pepper

I'd eat this every day and any day; it is delicious. I like to fry the soft tortilla in this recipe, making for a crisp, crunchy taco on which to serve this fiery chicken spiked with plenty of lime juice, and extra-hot sauce as always. The combination of the slaw, fried pumpkin seeds, coriander and spring onions is glorious alongside the chipotle chicken. You will need plenty of napkins to eat this!

1. Put the pumpkin seeds into a dry, non-stick frying pan. Over a moderate heat, dry fry the seeds until they toast and begin to crackle. Remove from the heat and keep to one side.

2. Mix the mayonnaise and sour cream together with the garlic and the chipotle paste to taste. Season well with salt and pepper and add half the lime juice. Use half this dressing to coat the leftover chicken. Reserve the remainder.

3. In a bowl, mix together the carrots, cabbage, spring onions (scallions) and coriander (cilantro). Add a big pinch of salt and the remaining lime juice. Mix well to coat.

4. One by one, warm the tortillas in a dry frying pan (or warm them in unison in the oven); or, if you like, add a splash of neutral oil to a frying pan over a moderate heat and fry the tortillas one by one, flipping carefully until they are golden on both sides – 1–2 minutes in total. Then, remove them from the heat and drain them on some kitchen paper – they will crisp up into tacos as they cool.

5. On each warm tortilla or taco, pile on some of the slaw and dressed chicken, then add some of the pumpkin seeds and finish with dollops of the remaining chipotle mayonnaise. Add hot sauce to taste and serve with lime wedges for squeezing.

Chicken with Mango, Tamarind, Peanuts and Chilli Sauce

Serves 4

3 tbsp pressed tamarind pulp, softened in the same quantity of boiling water to form a paste, discarding any seeds; or use tamarind paste or sauce

juice of 1 lime

1 tbsp light brown soft or palm sugar

1 tsp Southeast Asian chilli sauce; or use Indonesian sambal oelek, to taste

2 tsp fish sauce (or use light soy sauce)

400g (14oz) leftover cooked chicken meat, shredded or sliced

2 ripe mangoes or use green unripe, peeled, stoned and thinly sliced

150g (5½oz) beansprouts

1 cucumber, peeled and thinly sliced

½ bunch of spring onions (scallions), thinly sliced

100g (3½oz) roasted peanuts, crushed

1 small bunch of mint, leaves roughly chopped (or use Thai basil)

salt

I'm looking to Southeast Asia for inspiration for this salad. I have had equal success making this salad with both ripe mangoes and firm, green unripe mangoes, so do use either. Unripe, this salad will have a crunchy texture, which is no bad thing; ripe, well, you get the picture. Tamarind is a wonderful ingredient, from the tamarind tree. When the seed pods ripen, the soft fibrous pulp is fruity and sweet-sour, which suits the flavours in this dish very well - fruity, salty and sour all mixed together with the leftover chicken and a shower of invigorating mint.

1. Whisk together the tamarind with the lime juice, sugar and chilli sauce or sambal oelek. Add the fish sauce (or light soy sauce) and season to taste with salt, remembering that the fish sauce is also salty.

2. Use half this dressing to coat the leftover chicken.

3. Toss the sliced mango, beansprouts, cucumber and spring onions (scallions) with half the peanuts and the remaining dressing and arrange on a serving plate.

4. Top with the dressed leftover chicken, then scatter with the mint and the remaining peanuts to serve.

Chicken with Cannellini Beans and Tomatoes

Serves 4

3 tbsp red wine vinegar
1 red onion, thinly sliced or diced
2 garlic cloves, crushed
500g (1lb 2oz) cherry tomatoes, halved
2 tsp Dijon mustard
4 tbsp olive oil
¼–½ tsp dried red chilli flakes,
    to taste (optional)
½ celery heart (the pale, leafy inside
    of celery), thinly sliced
2 x 400g (14oz) cans of white beans
    (such as cannellini or haricot),
    drained and rinsed
50g (1¾oz) kalamata olives, pitted
1 small bunch of flat-leaf parsley,
    roughly chopped
400g (14oz) leftover cooked chicken
    meat, shredded or sliced
salt and freshly ground black pepper

With the leftover chicken good to go, this should take you about 5 minutes to pull together. Use any tinned white bean, though cannellini is a favourite for me, and choose ripe cherry tomatoes. This salad will only get better if left to wallow in its juices for an hour or so – just add the cold leftover chicken when you're ready to serve.

1. In a small bowl mix the vinegar with the red onion and leave the onion to macerate for at least 5 minutes.

2. Mix the garlic, tomatoes, mustard, olive oil and chilli flakes (if using) in another bowl, then mix in the macerated onion along with the celery heart, white beans, olives and parsley and season to taste with salt and pepper.

3. Arrange the salad and chicken on a platter.

Chicken with Tortilla Chips, Black Beans and Feta

Serves 4

1 small red onion, thinly sliced

boiling water from a kettle

2 limes: 1 juiced, 1 cut into wedges

400g (14oz) leftover cooked chicken meat, shredded or sliced

1–2 tsp chipotle paste, to taste (or use ancho chilli paste for a smokier flavour)

1 tbsp vegetable or olive oil

1 small garlic clove, finely chopped

1 tsp ground cumin

big pinch of smoked (or unsmoked) paprika

1 x 400g (14oz) can of black beans, drained and rinsed

150g (5½oz) tortilla chips

2 avocados, peeled, stoned and flesh diced small

50g (1¾oz) feta, crumbled (optional)

1–2 jalapeños, thinly sliced, to taste

1 small bunch of coriander (cilantro), leaves roughly chopped

salt and freshly ground black pepper

hot sauce or your choice, to serve

Another rapid-assembly chicken salad. Granted the pink pickled onion will take a few minutes to make, but other than that, this is effortless cooking – tortilla chips piled high with leftover chicken and black beans, all showered with chopped avocado, coriander and crumbled feta cheese. If you can source Mexican queso fresco instead of feta, then please do consider it. With Mexico in mind, be bold with the chipotle chilli paste, lime and fresh jalapeño; both the beans and the chicken will thank you for it.

1. Cover the onion in a bowl with boiling water and leave it for 5 minutes. Then drain, rinse under cold water and drain well. Add half the lime juice and a big pinch of salt. Put to one side.

2. Mix the chicken with the chipotle paste, oil, garlic, cumin and paprika until well coated, then stir through the black beans. Add the remaining lime juice and season well with salt and plenty of freshly ground black pepper.

3. On a large serving platter, pile the tortilla chips and top with the black bean and chicken mixture, before piling on the avocados, pickled red onion, crumbled feta, sliced jalapeños and chopped coriander (cilantro). Serve with extra lime wedges on the side to squeeze over, and your favourite hot sauce.

Fattoush with Chicken, Radish and Apricot

Serves 4

2 pita breads
75ml (2½fl oz) olive oil
½ small bunch of spring onions
  (scallions), trimmed and thinly sliced
150g (5½oz) daikon radish or pink
  radishes, thinly sliced
1 cucumber, peeled, deseeded and
  thinly sliced
2 small gem lettuces, thinly sliced
4 ripe apricots, stoned and thinly sliced
  or diced small (use 80g/2¾oz dried
  apricots, thinly sliced or diced, if fresh
  are out of season)
500g (1lb 2oz) ripe cherry tomatoes,
  halved
1 large bunch of flat-leaf parsley,
  leaves roughly chopped
1 small bunch of mint, leaves roughly
  chopped
½ small bunch of dill, leaves roughly
  chopped
400g (14oz) leftover cooked chicken
  meat, shredded or sliced
finely grated zest and juice of 1 lemon
1 garlic clove, finely crushed
2 tsp sumac powder
pinch of chilli flakes, or more to taste
  (optional)
1 tbsp sesame seeds or za'atar
salt and freshly ground black pepper

Fattoush is a Levantine or eastern Mediterranean recipe for chopped salad. There are many recipes for fattoush, from the simplest offering to the more convoluted, but the common theme is one of a vibrant, crunchy, herbaceous salad that can also include fresh fruit and stale or toasted pita or flat bread. I would encourage a certain amount of flexibility and confidence when making fattoush. I've used apricots, though peaches, cherries, nectarines or persimmons would all be gorgeous. As for salad ingredients, an assortment of thinly sliced or shredded celery heart, kohlrabi, white cabbage, fennel, carrot are all welcome, so use what you have to hand.

1. Preheat the oven to 180°C/160°C fan/350°F/Gas 4. Cut the pita breads into squares and toss them with 3 tablespoons of the olive oil in a baking tray. Bake them in the oven for 10 minutes, until toasted and golden. Put to one side.

2. Put all the sliced vegetables into a large bowl with the apricots, tomatoes and toasted pita and add the chopped herbs. Scatter the chicken on top.

3. To make a dressing, mix the zest and juice of the lemon with the remaining olive oil and add the crushed garlic to taste. Pour the dressing over the assembled salad and mix well, then check the seasoning.

4. Sprinkle the salad with the sumac and chilli flakes (if using) and finish with the sesame seeds or za'atar.

5. You can serve immediately or, if you'd rather, leave the fattoush for 30 minutes for the flavours to mingle and the pita to absorb the dressing – giving you a chewier rather than crisp pita texture in the finished salad.

Chicken Baguette with Tarragon, Gherkin and Mustard Butter

Serves 4

60g (2oz) butter, softened at room
   temperature
1 heaped tsp Dijon mustard
½ small bunch of tarragon, leaves picked
   and finely chopped
1 shallot, very finely diced
100g (3½oz) gherkins or cornichons,
   finely chopped
400g (14oz) leftover cooked chicken,
   shredded or sliced
1 fresh rustic baguette, the crustier
   the better
½–1 green lettuce, leaves separated
salt and freshly ground black pepper

You won't regret making this with your leftover chicken. Tarragon, Dijon mustard and shallot, not to mention the baguette, which must be good and crunchy, takes us to France for this final offering. Simplicity, for pure and unbridled chicken-eating joy – that is all.

1. Beat the butter in a small bowl until creamy, then add the mustard, tarragon, shallot and gherkins or cornichons. Season well to taste with salt and plenty of freshly ground black pepper.

2. Season the leftover chicken with salt and pepper to taste.

3. Slice the whole baguette along its length and spread over the flavoured butter. Arrange the lettuce leaves and well-seasoned chicken evenly along the length of the baguette.

4. Cut the baguette into 4 equal pieces and serve it like so, or wrap it for a picnic.

Index

Acknowledgements

We're a tight team when it comes to producing these cookbooks: my husband Matt, who helps with recipe development; our wonderful children Grace, Ivy and Dorothy (though two of these three were less cooperative when it came to recipe testing this book as they are vegetarian); Sam Folan the photographer, whom my kids all adore and is now a lifelong family friend (and Dot, his trusty assistant, when she can wangle the day off from school to help him). And that's it from here in Bristol on the shoot days. Faye Wears sends beautiful, thoughtful props from London, making all the food we cook on the day look utterly compelling; Harriet Webster, Claire Rochford and Sarah Lavelle are all on call to encourage and direct.

I am very lucky to call this my job. The shoot days are full of music, laughter and so much washing up, and the days spent writing are always in my kitchen with the clock ticking and my kids soon home from school. I wouldn't have it any other way.

Thanks to Netherton Foundry for driving from Shropshire to Bristol to deliver some of your incredible pans for the shoot – they are simply beautiful to cook in.

Thanks also to Pipers Farm for supplying all the chicken that we cooked for the book – properly free range.

Managing Director Sarah Lavelle
Commissioning Editor Harriet Webster
Copy-editor Judy Barratt
Assistant Editor Sofie Shearman
Head of Design Claire Rochford
Designer Gemma Hayden
Food Stylists Claire Thomson and
  Matt Williamson
Photographer Sam Folan
Prop Stylist Faye Wears
Head of Production Stephen Lang
Production Controller Sabeena Atchia

Published in 2023 by Quadrille,
an imprint of Hardie Grant Publishing

Quadrille
52–54 Southwark Street
London SE1 1UN
quadrille.com

Cataloguing in Publication Data:
a catalogue record for this book is available from The British Library.

Text © Claire Thomson 2023
Photography © Sam Folan 2023
Design © Quadrille 2023

ISBN 978 1 83783 088 6
Printed in China

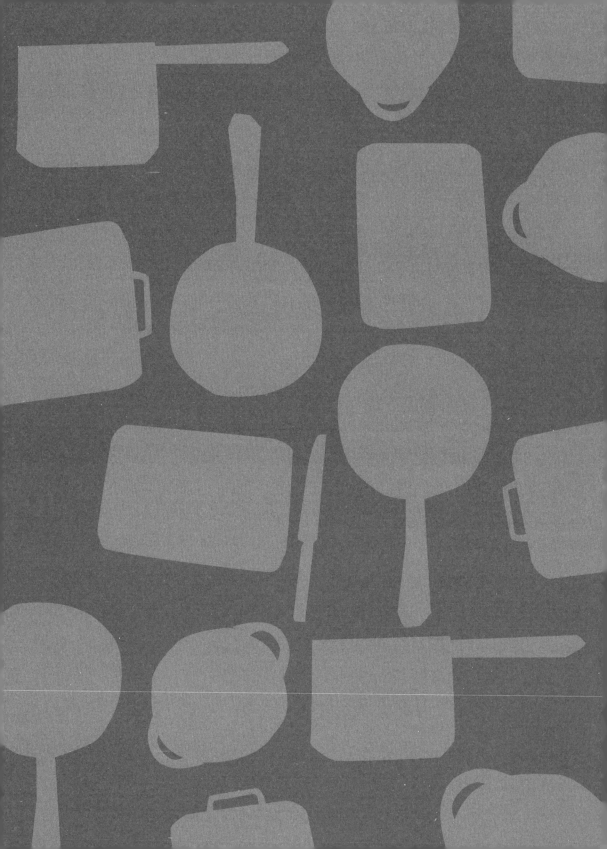